DragonKingKarl's 1983 Pro Wrestling Omnibus is taken from the *Ultimate History of Pro Wrestling - A Timeline of Every Major Event in Pro Wrestling History* which is an ongoing research project at WhenItWasCool.com and is the culmination of research by many of the greatest historians in pro wrestling. I make mention of several of these by name because, without their research and work, much of the history of wrestling would not be known.

They are: Steve Yohe (In my humble opinion the gold standard in wrestling historians), Mark Hewitt, J. Michael Kenyon (we own so much knowledge to the archives compiled by the late researcher), Norman Kietzer, James Melby, Royal Duncan, Gary Will, Jason Campbell (an unsung hero in wrestling research), John Arezzi, Bill Apter (I grew up on the newsstand magazines and he and George have my full respect and appreciation), George Napolitano (ditto what I said about Apter), Libnan Ayoub, Gherardo Bonini, Mike Chapman, Hisaharu Tanabe, Don Luce, Dave Meltzer (I literally would not have had a long history in wrestling publishing without Dave), Bryan Alvarez (My friend and a great guy), Bruce Mitchell, Seth Hanson, Joseph Svinth, Tom Burke, Dan Cerquitella, Vance Nevada (another unsung hero of wrestling research), Robert Rothhaas, Greg Oliver, Evan Ginzburg, Tim Hornbaker, Matt Farmer, David Williamson, Beau James (the undisputed professor of southern wrestling knowledge), Chris Charlton, Mike Sempervive (my friend and a great podcasters), John Perlin, Mark James (I love Mark's many books), Graham Cawthon (same for Graham, great historical work), Richard Land, Joseph Shedlock, Eddie Gilbert (the late wrestling star started out publishing bulletins and fanzines from which I still draw research), William Schutte, Kris Zellner, David Bix, Scott Bowden, Jim Cornette, Brian Last (Brian

Last has dug up a lot of very interesting wrestling history and continues to chronicle it via his podcast network), Juan Nunez (many of you many not know Juan, but he is a tremendous resource for knowledge. I am very grateful to have had his input on various projects), DA White, Ron Fuller (Welch), Scott Teal (any book by Scott Teal is well worth your time reading), Paul Sosnowski (Paul has been a invaluable resource in fact checking and adding to our *Ultimate History of Pro Wrestling Timeline*), Keith Shewchuck, Terry Justice, Ken Zimmerman, Jr., Dick Bourne, Dave Millican, Jimmy Wheeler, Fumi Saito, Jim Valley (another of the true good guys of wrestling and my "go-to" for information on Pacific Northwest information), Evan Ginzburg, Randy Hales, Dale Pierce, Norman Dooley, Tom Burke, John Clark, Don Laible, Chris Jericho, Georgiann Makropoulos, Mike Rodgers, Rich Tate, Burt Ray, James Zordani (what would we historians do without the research of the late "Clawmaster"?), Warren Styles (a true supporter of When It Was Cool), Andy Cohen (I couldn't do When It Was Cool without Andy who has been great to us), NoFriender (my mysterious friend), Eric Darsie (a foundational rock for When It Was Cool), Von Davis (my brother from another mother), Dan Madigan, George Lentz, Aaron Gartlan (a great source of Continental love and information), Rock Rims, Jim Burgett, Andrew Calvert, Al Getz (great historian), James Guttman, Ethan Tyler (when I fill out my Wrestling Observer Hall of Fame ballot, it is Ethan's opinion I most value), Farid Azam, Phil Lions, Pat Laprade (thank you for your help), and many others.

The items considered for this timeline include: Any major pro wrestling show with an attendance of 5,000 or more people, or a show with historical significance. Title changes, arrests or documented legal incidents, birthdays, deaths, major angles, or any event which would be considered of historical importance.

If you enjoy the contents of this book, you can find more content similar to it at our website WhenItWasCool.com and if you find that information useful, fun, and interesting, I hope you will consider supporting us on Patreon. There are multiple links on the front page of the website. I have tried to use the platform at When It Was Cool to keep pro wrestling history alive and correctly chronicled but in doing so we really need your support. We have over 2000 podcasts, many dealing with the history of professional wrestling available for people to listen to as soon as they sign up. Plus, we have a substantial number of archival pro wrestling footage on our YouTube channel which cannot be monetized via YouTube. However, we hope you will support WhenItWasCool.com on Patreon to help us continue to chronicle professional wrestling's history, without bias, kayfabe, or agenda.

Finally, before diving into the world of professional wrestling in 1983, I'd like to personally thank Bryan Alvarez and Dave Meltzer who have kindly given me a platform for over ten years to discuss and research pro wrestling history at their stellar WrestlingObserver.com where I host the *DragonKingKarl Classic Wrestling Audio Show*. Dave Meltzer is indisputably the greatest pro wrestling journalist ever and his contributions to keeping pro wrestling history alive can not be understated. Bryan Alvarez has been a true friend and honestly one of the nicest people in the world. He deserves all the success that comes his way at the Wrestling Observer / Figure Four Online empire.

Special, special thanks to my wife Tonya who is the foundation upon which When It Was Cool is built and my most special person in the entire world.

Now... Let's Talk About Professional Wrestling in 1983:

In 1983 I had already been a fan of pro wrestling for a few years. I was born in 1971 and I am honestly not sure what my first memory of pro wrestling is. Growing up in rural north Alabama, pro wrestling was more than a television show, or an event, it was part of the culture. Here in Alabama, we didn't (and still don't) have any professional sports teams. The closest thing we have to a "home team" or pro sports franchise is NCAA football and University of Alabama Crimson Tide football team. NCAA football in Alabama is second only to religion in cultural importance.

With the lack of a professional football, baseball, or basketball team, that left an entertainment gap and during the 1960s through the 1980s, that gap was filled by pro wrestling. I grew up in the post-Vietnam era. Kids of my age group around here still played soldier using sticks or toy guns. We grew up on the Six Million Dollar Man, G.I. Joe, comic books, and probably the biggest franchise of my lifetime hit pop culture in 1977: Star Wars. During those formative years, I often listened to adults passionately discuss memories of people like Tojo Yamamoto, The Interns, The Medics, and more.

My Grandfather was a pro wrestling fan and I can remember him sitting in his favorite chair watching it on television. My aunt and uncle would even occasionally go to the wrestling cards in Birmingham, Alabama (or closer if possible, Birmingham being over an hour away). But I, personally, don't remember when I first started paying close attention to pro wrestling but it was probably around 1978 or 1979.

I do, however, remember when pro wrestling became the most important thing to me, as far as entertainment goes. That would have been in the later part of 1981. It seems like, at that time, pro wrestling started really heating up around here, centered mainly around our "home team" territory which was Ron Fuller's Southeastern Championship Wrestling (SECW). As all the kids in the neighborhood would gather to play, it was usually football, baseball, or acting out superhero drama, or various war games through the north Alabama woods, around late 1981 my friends started talking more and more about pro wrestling and the various characters such as Ron Fuller, Bob Armstrong, Jimmy Golden, Mr. Olympia, Ken Lucas, and The Sheepherders.

Wanting to fit in, I began watching Southeastern Championship Wrestling for myself on Saturday mornings out of the Birmingham television market. I was quickly hooked. I loved comic books. I learned to read on comic books, so masked men doing heroic feats and muscular giants fighting was nothing new to me but this was real life (sort of)! I immediately was enthralled by the wrestlers who were somewhat superhuman looking. There was Austin Idol with his white blonde hair, incredible muscles, and could cut a blistering interview. There was Ron Fuller, all six-feet-nine-inches tall and utterly hateable... sometimes. There was "Bullet" Bob Armstrong, the local hero. A former Marine and Firefighter. How can you possibly hate that? Well, come 1983 you would certainly hate him, but hang on, we will get to that.

My favorite pro wrestler, however, was a masked man called Mr. Olympia. He was a good guy (babyface) at the time and wore the glittery masks, often with a matching jacket, and he seemed like a superhero straight out of the pages of a comic book. He forever became my "favorite wrestler". Many years later, after I had done some wrestling and promoting myself, I met the man who was Mr. Olympia under the mask, Jerry Stubbs. I was introduced to him at a nostalgia show by way of a friend I had met in wrestling named Ron West. I didn't tell Jerry Stubbs any of this, mind you, for fear of looking like an absolute idiot, but he was my childhood hero and I felt accomplished.

By 1982 I was "all-in" for pro wrestling. Much to my pleasure, I discovered that not only could I watch Southeastern Championship Wrestling on television but, from where I lived in the northwest corner of the state, I could also get Memphis CWA wrestling out of the Tupelo television market. From there I was introduced to another person who became one of my favorites, Jerry "The King" Lawler, along with Dutch Mantel, Bill Dundee, and hey, there's Austin Idol again! I was collecting and reading comic books less and less and wrestling magazines more and more.

It was in those magazines I learned about Hulk Hogan (who, in 1982 would rise to pop culture fame in Rocky III), Nick Bockwinkel, Bruiser Brody, Tommy "Wildfire" Rich, Bob Backlund, Harley Race, and learn about wrestlers from other countries like another colorful superhero like character Mil Mascaras and Japanese wrestlers like Giant Baba and Antonio Inoki. I was hooked.

Then came "Nature Boy" Ric Flair. I probably first saw Ric Flair in one of the numerous newsstand magazines at the time. Like Austin Idol, he had white blonde hair and talked a great game. Heck, he talked the GREATEST game! When he finally came to Southeastern wrestling and began taking on my local heroes, I was caught, hook-line-and-sinker into a life of pro wrestling fandom.

Which brings us to 1983. Since my childhood, I have watched, researched, and chronicled pro wrestling history. In the early 2000s, based on research I did in the old DragonKing Press Newsletter (available in the Patron archives at WhenItWasCool.com), I was hired by a group of attorneys in Atlanta, GA to do research for a lawsuit they had filed against Turner Sports, the parent company of World Championship Wrestling (WCW) for discrimination. My job was to compile statistics about whatever they requested. This caused me to be court certified as a "pro wrestling expert" in the State of Georgia. WCW, by the way, settled the lawsuit, though doubtfully due to my research and more likely as a way to keep the accusations out of the press and out of court.

By 1983 I knew every wrestler, every storyline, and bought every wrestling magazine I could afford. I walked, talked, and breathed pro wrestling (just like most everyone else around here). My Star Wars and G.I. Joe action figures were no longer fighting evil in space or the terrorist organization known as Cobra. Instead, they were wearing wrestling "belts" made out of bread ties threaded through gold buttons from my grandma's sewing basket, wearing "masks" made out of (ironically) masking tape, and wearing capes, robes, and jackets made out of whatever I could find to make them out of. Luke Skywalker was no longer the future of the Jedi Order, he was an upcoming babyface at my kitchen table much to the dismay of Cobra Commander.

So many important things were coming together in 1983 which would push pro wrestling to the top of the pop culture ladder. The foundation blocks of the WWF national expansion were being laid by Vince McMahon with his purchase of the company from his father. Later, he would acquire Hulk Hogan who would start 1983 as a top star in the AWA and New Japan Pro Wrestling (where he would also become their first IWGP champion) and end the year in the WWF prepping to become the WWF champion. The years-long WWF title reign of Bob Backlund would come to an end and transition to the Iron Sheik at the end of the year.

Fans in Memphis began 1983 believing and being told on television that Jerry "The King" Lawler was the AWA World heavyweight champion having defeated Nick Bockwinkel at the end of 1982, however, it was not to be. The AWA World title was only officially "held up" in Memphis and Nick Bockwinkel was still the champion everywhere else and would be again in Memphis as well. Crowds were up and down in Memphis all year.

Sgt. Slaughter had left Jim Crockett Promotions along with his partner Don Kernodle for the WWF. However, the WWF did nothing of note with Kernodle and Sgt. Slaughter would eventually leave as well after a dispute of merchandising rights, especially his action figure.

World Class Championship Wrestling (WCCW) in Texas was still red hot with David Von Erich presumed to be a future, if not the next, NWA World heavyweight champion. However, David would die in a Japanese hotel room in 1984. The Freebirds remained a hot act, but the death of David Von Erich would be the first crack to form in the juggernaut World Class promotion.

Georgia Championship Wrestling would see the formation of The Road Warriors, the "Last Battle of Atlanta " focused on the long running Tommy Rich verses Buzz Sawyer feud which would go down in wrestling history.

Mid-South wrestling was red hot drawing huge crowds to the New Orleans Superdome and the international scene was strong with New Japan Pro Wrestling's IWGP tournament, huge crowds in Mexico, and more. 1983 was a majorly important year in pro wrestling.

Abbreviations:

AWA - American Wrestling Association (Verne Gagne promotion)

EMLL / CMLL - Empresa Mexicana de Lucha Libre

JCP - Jim Crockett Promotions Mid-Atlantic Territory

Memphis - CWA - Jerry Jarrett's Memphis based promotion

NJPW - New Japan Pro Wrestling

NWA - National Wrestling Alliance

Saga of the Death of David Von Erich - Refers to a podcast series by When It Was Cool Wrestling (available on all major podcast apps or directly from WhenItWasCool.com) detailing the last several months of the life of David Von Erich (David Adkisson) up to his death in 1984.

SECW - Southeastern Championship Wrestling (Ron Fuller promotion)

PNW - Pacific Northwest Wrestling (Don Owen promotion)

UWA - Universal Wrestling Association (Mexican wrestling promotion)

WWC - World Wrestling Council (Puerto Rico)

WWF - World Wrestling Federation (today's WWE)

The Timeline of Professional Wrestling in 1983

With Various "DragonKingKarl" Historical Notes Included

January 1983

01-01-1983: Norman Fredrick Charles III won the vacant NWA U.S. Junior title in a tournament in Dothan, AL for the Southeastern Championship Wrestling promotion (SECW).

Central States: St. Louis, MO: Attendance: 11,029 sell out: Manny Fernandez & Mark Romero defeated Jerry Brown & Kim Duk… Rick Martel pinned Roger Kirby… Bobby Duncum pinned Mike George… Greg Valentine & Bob Orton Jr. defeated Dick the Bruiser & Bob Brown… Bruiser Brody pinned Crusher (Hercules) Ayala… Kerry Von Erich defeated NWA Missouri heavyweight champion Harley Race via DQ… NWA World champion Ric Flair pinned Butch Reed.

In San Antonio, TX Tully Blanchard defeated Bob Sweetan to win the Southwestern title in a tournament.

Rip Oliver & The Assassin (David Sierra) defeated Jack & Stan Stasiak for the Pacific Northwest tag team titles in Portland, OR.

01-02-1983: In Memphis, TN at the Mid-South Coliseum in front of 4,111 fans Jerry Roberts (Jacques Rougeau) defeated Sabu (Coco Samoa) for the Mid-America title.

01-03-1983: In West Palm Beach, FL Barry Windham defeated NWA World heavyweight champion Ric Flair by DQ.

Great Kabuki wins the World Class TV title from Al Madril in Fort Worth, TX.

01-04-1983: On the WWF Championship Wrestling TV taping, WWF champion Bob Backlund debuts a new world championship belt. The short-lived **green title belt** with round face plate on Buddy Rogers' Rogers' Corner segment.

DragonKingKarl Note: The belt dubbed "Big Green" by wrestling belt historians was short-lived and, supposedly, thrown away outside an unspecified arena in a dumpster following the creation of the new belt in 1984. Big Green is notable for being the championship belt that came with the Hulk Hogan LJN action figure.

In Tampa, FL Barry Windham defeated NWA World heavyweight champion Ric Flair by DQ.

El Canek verses Dos Caras for the UWA World Title at El Toreo de Cuatro Caminos, Naucalpan, México draws 18,000 fans.

01-05-1983: In Miami Beach, FL The Kangaroos (Don Kent & Johnny Heffernan) defeated Ron Bass & Barry Windham to win the Global tag team titles. Also, NWA World heavyweight champion Ric Flair defeated Rufus R. Jones by DQ.

01-06-1983: World Wrestling Council (WWC) World champion Carlos Colon pinned NWA World champion Ric Flair in a non-title match in San Juan, Puerto Rico. The show draws 12,000 fans.

Rip Oliver wins the annual Salem City, Oregon championship tournament defeating Chris Adams in the finals.

01-08-1983: Don Muraco defeated WWF champion Bob Backlund by count out at Landover, MD Capital Centre. The show draws 19,800 fans.

Carlos Colon & Invader 1 (Jose Gonzalez) verses Ric Flair & Terry Funk in Bayamon, Puerto Rico draws 14,000 fans.

Georgia Championship Wrestling: At the Omni in Atlanta, GA: Butch Reed won a two ring battle royal… Stan Hansen & Tommy Rich defeated The Moondogs (Rex & Spot)… Judy Martin won a battle royal… Paul Orndorff defeated Super Destroyer (Scott Irwin)… Tito Santana defeated Iron Sheik by count out… Kandi Malloy defeated Judy Martin… Joe Lightfoot defeated Chick Donovan.

In Jackson, TN Rick McGraw breaks his ankle. He was teaming with the Dream Machine (Troy Graham) at the time and were the WWA World tag team champions. The titles are vacated.

Tunney Promotions: In Toronto, Canada with an attendance of 18,237: King Parsons defeated Jerry Bryant… Private Jim Nelson (AKA: Boris Zhukoff) defeated Nick DeCarlo… Rudy & Terry Kay defeated **Ken Timbs** & Frank Monte… Salvatore Bellomo defeated Buddy Rose by DQ… Ray Stevens defeated Jimmy Snuka by count out… Angelo Mosca defeated Leroy Brown in a Steel Cage match to retain the Canadian title… Leo Burke defeated Johnny Weaver in a Steel Cage match to retain the North American title.

DragonKingKarl Note: When I began running my own independent wrestling promotion in the early to mid-1990's, Ken Timbs was one of the people I used. I managed Ken Timbs on shows and he taught me a lot about the wrestling business. While I was technically "trained" by other people, it is Ken Timbs who I most fondly remember as my mentor in the wrestling business. He was a true professional, a dedicated family man, and highly experienced. Over the years, I have often been asked about the "DragonKingKarl Stern" name. I owe most of that to Ken Timbs. Karl Stern (spoiler alert) is not my real legal name. When I went to manage Ken Timbs in a match for the first time he told me, you need a different name, to which he said was to be "Karl Stern". Fine, I guess I am Karl Stern now. The "DragonKing" part came later. On another show there was a wrestler doing an Ultimo Dragon knock off gimmick with a generic name. During this time period, the original Tiger Mask (Satoru Sayama) was wrestling under the name "Tiger King" in Japan. Ken Timbs began coming up with other "knock off" or "Value Brand" names for other wrestlers sitting around the dressing room and mine was... you guessed it... DragonKing. Mind you, I am six-foot-three and around 250 pounds and resembled nothing of Satoru Sayama and sure as hell couldn't wrestle like him, but there I was, wearing, ironically an Ultimo Dragon mask we were selling at a gimmick table as DragonKing. I never wrestled, nor promoted, nor ever appeared as "DragonKing" but I kind of liked the name and when I launched the history based *DragonKing Press Newsletter* (available to Patreon members at WhenItWasCool.com) I kept the name alive and have ever since. Now you know the origin of the name DragonKingKarl.

01-09-1983: In a rematch of a December 19, 1982 match at a sold out Palacio de Deportes in Santo Domingo in the Dominican Republic, **Jack Veneno** (Rafael Sanchez), billed as the defending NWA World heavyweight champion, defeated Ric Flair (recognized everywhere else as NWA World heavyweight champion) via DQ when Roddy Piper interfered.

DragonKingKarl Note: Some time after this match it was announced in the Dominican Republic that Jack Veneno was stripped of the championship for not wanting to leave the country and defend it. The story was the Dominican Republic was going through troubled times and a lot of corruption, and Veneno said he didn't think it was right to leave the country and his fans during those tough times. Most title histories do not recognize Jack Veneno as a former world champion or, at least, mention his name in the footnotes. However, video of the Jack Veneno title win was included in a documentary about him several years ago released in the Dominican Republic and clearly shows Jack Veneno defeating Ric Flair. A very interesting footnote in the history of the National Wrestling Alliance World heavyweight championship and something most people, in 1983, were not aware had happened.

01-10-1983: Robert Gibson defeated Norman Frederick Charles III to win the NWA U.S. Junior title for Southeastern Wrestling.

In Memphis, TN at the Mid-South Coliseum in front of a crowd of 8,208 fans Nick Bockwinkel defeated Jerry Lawler to regain the disputed AWA World heavyweight title. AWA never actually recognized the December 1982 AWA World title change and Memphis television danced around the situation insinuating that Jerry Lawler was the champion yet, at the same time, having him surrender the title on television to Eddie Marlin to "hold" until the rematch or Bockwinkel refused to wrestle. During this match and leading to the finish the "injured" Jimmy Hart appeared at ringside beside a man wrapped up in medical gauze whom it was assumed was Hart. Instead, it turned out to be Andy Kauffman which distracted Lawler allowing Bockwinkel to grab a pin and "regain" the title.

In West Palm Beach, FL at the Auditorium: NWA World heavyweight champion Ric Flair defeated Barry Windham.

The Destroyer (Dick Beyer) defeated Billy Robinson for the International championship in Quebec, Canada. Also, Tony Parisi & Gino Brito defeated Pat Patterson & Pierre Lefebvre for the International tag team titles.

01-11-1983: A mask verses money match takes place at the Ft. Hesterly Armory in Tampa, FL. The Midnight Rider (Dusty Rhodes) & Barry Windham defeat NWA World champion Ric Flair & Kevin Sullivan when the Midnight Rider pins Ric Flair. On the same show Terry Allen (AKA: Magnum TA) & Scott McGhee defeated The Kangaroos (Don Kent & Johnny Heffernan) to win the Global tag team titles.

01-13-1983: Hulk Hogan verses Ken Patera at the Salt Palace, Salt Lake City, UT draws 10,000 fans. Bobby Heenan battled Buck Zumhofe to a draw... Wahoo McDaniel defeated Jacques Rene Goulet... Jesse Ventura defeated Baron Von Raschke... Crusher Blackwell & Adnan El Kaissey defeated Rick Martel & Steve Olsonoski... Hulk Hogan defeated Ken Patera via DQ.

01-14-1983: WWF: Pittsburgh, PA: Civic Arena: Attendance: 14,000: Tony Garea pinned Baron Mikel Scicluna... Mr. Fuji pinned SD Jones... Don Muraco defeated WWF champion Bob Backlund via count-out... Ray Stevens & Buddy Rose defeated Jimmy Snuka & Rocky Johnson via DQ... Salvatore Bellomo pinned Charlie Fulton... Superstar Billy Graham fought WWF Intercontinental champion Pedro Morales to a double count-out... WWF tag team champions Chief Jay & Jules Strongbow defeated the Wild Samoans (Afa & Sika) via DQ.

In Ft. Pierce, FL Midnight Rider (Dusty Rhodes) defeated NWA World heavyweight champion Ric Flair but did not win the title.

Sam Houston Coliseum, Houston, TX draws 10,000 fans. Tim Horner defeated Buddy Landel… Tiger Conway, Jr. defeated Kelly Kiniski… Steve Williams defeated Marty Lunde (Soon to be known as: Arn Anderson)… Dick Murdoch & Tom Prichard defeated The Grapplers (Len Denton & Tony Anthony)… Chavo Guerrero defeated Gino Hernandez… Tony Atlas & Mr. Wrestling II (Johnny Walker) & Stagger Lee (Junkyard Dog) defeated Matt Borne & Ted DiBiase & Jim Duggan… **Kamala** won a two ring battle royal.

AWA in Denver, CO: Bobby Heenan battled Buck Zumhofe to a draw… Wahoo McDaniel beat Sgt. Rene Goulet… Rick Martel beat Ken Patera… Hulk Hogan beat Jesse Ventura by DQ… Greg Gagne & Jim Brunzell beat Jerry Blackwell & Sheik Adnan Al Kaissey in a steel cage match.

DragonKingKarl Note: James Harris was known most famously in pro wrestling as Kamala the Ugandan Giant. Early on, the name was spelled "Kimala" instead. I have opted to use the better known spelling of "Kamala" for website search purposes.

01-15-1983: Norman Fredrick Charles III fought Robert Gibson to a disputed finish, thus, the NWA U.S. Junior title was held up for Southeastern Wrestling (SECW).

WWF: Boston, MA: Boston Garden: Attendance: 14,780: Tony Altimore defeated Fred Marzino… Eddie Gilbert defeated Pete Doherty… Salvatore Bellomo defeated Swede Hanson... Don Muraco defeated WWF champion Bob Backlund via count-out... WWF tag team champions Chief Jay & Jules Strongbow fought the Wild Samoans (Afa & Sika) to a draw... Superstar Billy Graham defeated WWF Intercontinental champion Pedro Morales via DQ... Jimmy Snuka & Rocky Johnson defeated Buddy Rose & Ray Stevens.

In Tampa, FL: NWA World heavyweight champion Ric Flair defeated Barry Windham.

In San Antonio, TX The Grapplers (Len Denton & Tony Anthony) defeated Ricky Morton & Ken Lucas to win the Southwest tag team titles.

AWA in Chicago, IL: Buck Zumhofe beat Tom Lintz... Jerry Lawler beat Tom Stone... Wahoo McDaniel beat Sgt. Rene Goulet... Ken Patera & Bobby Duncum beat Rick Martel & Steve O... Hulk Hogan beat Jesse Ventura by DQ... Jerry Blackwell & Sheik Adnan Al Kaissey beat Jim Brunzell & Mad Dog Vachon.

01-16-1983: Hulk Hogan & Mad Dog Vachon defeated Jesse Ventura & Ken Patera and AWA World heavyweight champion Nick Bockwinkel defeated Rick Martel by DQ at the Civic Center, St. Paul MN, drawing 17,000 fans. Buck Zumhofe battled Bobby Heenan to a draw... Jerry Blackwell beat Steve O... Sgt. Rene Goulet beat Baron Von Raschke... Wahoo McDaniel beat Bobby Duncum.

01-17-1983: In Memphis, TN: Mid-South Coliseum drawing 5,690: Bobby Fulton beat Carl Fergie... Dutch Mantel pinned The Angel... Jesse Barr beat Ken Raper... Carl Fergie & The Angel & Jesse Barr beat Dutch Mantel & Bobby Fulton & Ken Raper... Stan Lane beat Jonathan Boyd via DQ... Bill Dundee &

Terry Taylor beat Adrian Street & Apocalypse (Mike Boyer)... The Fabulous Ones (Steve Keirn & Stan Lane) beat The Sheepherders (Jonathan Boyd & Luke Williams) via forfeit to win the Southern tag team titles... Bobby Eaton & Sabu (Coco Samoa) beat Jerry Lawler & Sweet Brown Sugar (Koko Ware) via DQ.

Robert Gibson defeated Norman Frederick Charles III to win the held up NWA U.S. Junior title for Southeastern Championship Wrestling in Birmingham, AL for SECW.

01-18-1983: The Kangaroos (Don Kent & Johnny Heffernan) defeated Terry Allen & Scott McGhee to win the Global tag team titles.

01-19-1983: In an incident that would have even more chilling ramifications later this year, Jimmy Snuka is arrested by Onondaga County, NY Sheriff's deputies following a domestic violence incident with Nancy Argentino. Argentino would be killed under suspicious circumstances later this same year and shortly before Snuka's death he would be indicted for her murder.

01-21-1983: Butch Reed defeated NWA World heavyweight champion Ric Flair in a $5000 challenge match in Chillicothe, MO for the Central States promotion. The title is not on the line.

Terry Gordy defeated Kevin Von Erich to win the World Class American heavyweight title in Dallas, TX.

01-22-1983: WWF in New York City, NY at Madison Square Garden. Attendance: 15,000. Results: Johnny Rodz defeated Pete Sanchez... SD Jones defeated Baron

Mikel Scicluna... Superstar Billy Graham defeated Swede Hanson... Don Muraco defeated WWF Intercontinental champion Pedro Morales to win the title... The Wild Samoans (Afa & Sika) managed by Captain Lou Albano defeated Tony Garea & Eddie Gilbert... Ray Stevens defeated Jules Strongbow... WWF champion Bob Backlund defeated Big John Studd... Jimmy Snuka managed by Buddy Rogers defeated Buddy Rose managed by Lou Albano... Salvatore Bellomo defeated Charlie Fulton... Rocky Johnson defeated Mr. Fuji.

01-23-1983: Dory Funk, Jr. defeated Jack Brisco for the NWA Mid-Atlantic title in Charlotte, NC. for Jim Crockett Promotions.

GCW at the Omni in Atlanta, GA in a non-title $5,000 challenge match Butch Reed defeated the NWA World heavyweight champion Ric Flair... Ole Anderson & Buzz Sawyer defeated Tommy Rich & Stan Hansen... Paul Orndorff defeated Ivan Koloff... Bruiser Brody defeated Tito Santana... Ray Candy battled Super Destroyer (Scott Irwin)... The Moondogs (Rex & Spot) defeated Joe Lightfoot & Tom Prichard... Paul Ellering defeated Johnny Rich... Brad Armstrong defeated Chick Donovan.

In Toronto, Canada at the Maple Leaf Gardens (Tunney Promotion) with an attendance of 11,309: Billy Red Lyons defeated Jerry Bryant... Johnny Weaver defeated Tim Gerrard... The Destroyer (Dick Beyer) & Bobby Bass defeated Rudy & Terry Kay... Leo Burke battled Tony Parisi to a draw... Big John Studd defeated Tony Garea... Jimmy Snuka defeated Ray Stevens with Salvatore Bellomo as special referee... Ricky Steamboat & Jay Youngblood defeated Sgt. Slaughter & Don Kernodle by DQ.

01-24-1983: In Memphis, TN: Mid-South Coliseum drawing 5,589: The Angel (Frank Morrell) beat Bobby Fulton… Jesse Barr wrestled **King Cobra** to a draw… Dutch Mantel pinned Carl Fergie… Southern tag team champions The Fabulous Ones (Steve Keirn & Stan Lane) beat Jonathon Boyd & The Angel… Bill Dundee & Terry Taylor beat Adrian Street & Apocalypse (Mike Boyer) in a no DQ match… Bobby Eaton & Sabu (Coco Samoa) beat Sweet Brown Sugar (Koko Ware) & Jerry Lawler in a no DQ match.

DragonKingKarl Note: King Cobra (James Kimbell) was a full time welder in Mississippi and wrestled semi-regularly in Memphis, Mid-South, and various Mississippi based independent wrestling groups. James Kimbell invented a device for cleaning garbage trucks that ended up making him a lot of money. In fifty-five years of working for the Republic Services company, he only missed one day of work due to a broken leg.

01-25-1983: Ivan Koloff returns to the WWF defeating Barry Hart (Barry Horowitz) in Allentown, PA at the Agricultural Hall and later Jeff Craney, Frankie Williams, and Miguel Feliciano on the same show. WWF champion Bob Backlund performed the Harvard Step test for an entire hour during the show. In a dark match following the TV tapings WWF champion Bob Backlund defeated Buddy Rose who was a substitute for Superstar Billy Graham.

The Fabulous Kangaroos (Don Kent & Johnny Heffernan) defeated Scott McGhee & Terry Allen in Tampa, FL to regain the Global tag team titles.

01-29-1983: WWF: Baltimore, MD: Civic Center: Attendance: 12,200: Pete Sanchez defeated Baron Mikel Scicluna... Eddie Gilbert defeated Charlie Fulton... Salvatore Bellomo defeated Johnny Rodz... Big John Studd defeated SD Jones... Swede Hanson defeated Curt Hennig... WWF tag team champions Chief Jay & Jules Strongbow fought the Wild Samoans (Afa & Sika) to a double DQ... Rocky Johnson defeated Superstar Billy Graham via DQ... Jimmy Snuka defeated Ray Stevens via count-out... Andre the Giant & Pedro Morales defeated WWF Intercontinental champion Don Muraco & Mr. Fuji... WWF champion Bob Backlund defeated Buddy Rose.

01-30-1983: In Memphis, TN: Mid-South Coliseum drawing 5,907: King Cobra beat Masked Marauder 1 (Sammy Holt)... The Angel (Frank Morrell) beat Phillip Rougeau... Apocalypse (Mike Boyer) beat Bobby Fulton... Big Red beat Marauder 2 (Ken Raper)... Dutch Mantel drew Jesse Barr... Dutch Mantel & Bobby Fulton & King Cobra & Big Red beat The Marauders & The Angel & Jesse Barr... Jerry Roberts (Jacques Rougeau) pinned Terry Taylor to win the Southern title... The Sheepherders (Jonathan Boyd & Luke Williams) beat The Fabulous Ones (Steve Keirn & Stan Lane) to win the Southern tag team titles in a loser leaves town vs. title match... Adrian Street beat Bill Dundee via DQ in a loser receiving ten lashes match... Jerry Lawler & Terry Funk & Sweet Brown Sugar (Koko Ware) beat Bobby Eaton & Sabu (Coco Samoa) & Carl Fergie in a Texas tornado death match.

February 1983

02-05-1983: WWF: Boston, MA: Boston Garden: Attendance: 14,810: Mr. Fuji defeated Pete Sanchez... Salvatore Bellomo defeated Charlie Fulton... Johnny Rodz defeated Baron Mikel Scicluna... Swede Hanson defeated Mac Rivera... WWF champion Bob Backlund fought WWF Intercontinental champion Don Muraco to a double DQ... WWF tag team champions Chief Jay & Jules Strongbow defeated the Wild Samoans (Afa & Sika)... Big John Studd defeated Tony Garea... Jimmy Snuka defeated Ray Stevens... Rocky Johnson defeated Superstar Billy Graham via DQ.

02-06-1983: In Memphis, TN at the Cook Convention Center in front of 3,206 fans The Fabulous Ones (Steve Keirn & Stan Lane) defeated The Sheepherders (Jonathan Boyd & Luke Williams) to win the Southern tag team titles.

At the Omni in Atlanta, GA: Iron Sheik defeated Dick Murdoch in an Iranian Club Challenge... Butch Reed battled Ivan Koloff to a draw... Bunkhouse Match: Stan Hansen defeated Ole Anderson... Dick Murdoch defeated Super Destroyer (Scott Irwin)... Paul Orndorff defeated Iron Sheik... Ray Candy defeated Bruiser Brody by DQ... Bob Roop defeated Brad Armstrong... Buzz Sawyer defeated Tommy Rich... The Moondogs (Rex & Spot) defeated Tito Santana & Joe Lightfoot... Paul Ellering defeated Tom Prichard.

AWA in Denver, CO: Buck Zumhofe beat Tom Lintz... Jerry Blackwell & Sheik Adnan Al Kaissey beat Baron Von Raschke & Mad Dog Vachon... Rene Goulet battled Steve O to a draw... Wahoo McDaniel beat Bobby Duncum... AWA World heavyweight champion Nick Bockwinkel beat Rick Martel.

02-07-1983: New Japan Pro Wrestling: in Tokyo, Japan: Sumo Hall: Shown February 11, 1983 on TV: Yoshiaki Fujiwara beat Yokpalsan... Kuniaki Kobayashi & Gran Hamada beat Kantaro Hoshino & Masanobu Kurisu... Osamu Kido beat Carlos Jose Estrada... Mike George beat Ryuma Go... Masa Saito beat Kengo Kimura... Hulk Hogan beat Blackjack Mulligan... WWF Junior Heavyweight champion Tiger Mask (Satoru Sayama) beat Black Tiger... Seiji Sakaguchi & Tatsumi Fujinami battled Riki Choshu & Killer Khan to a double count out... Rusher Kimura & Animal Hamaguchi & Isamu Teranishi beat Antonio Inoki in a handicap match.

In Louisville, KY The Sheepherders (Jonathan Boyd & Luke Williams) regained the Southern tag team titles from the Fabulous Ones (Steve Keirn & Stan Lane)

Pro wrestling announcer Marty O'Neill dies at the age of 75.

02-08-1983: WWF: Buffalo, NY: Attendance: 9,200: Salvatore Bellomo defeated Charlie Fulton... Swede Hanson defeated Curt Hennig... Mr. Fuji fought Chief Jay Strongbow to a draw... The Wild Samoans (Afa & Sika) defeated Tony Garea & Eddie Gilbert... Big John Studd defeated Jules Strongbow... Rocky Johnson defeated Buddy Rose... Pedro Morales defeated Superstar Billy Graham via count-out... Jimmy Snuka defeated Ray Stevens... WWF champion Bob Backlund fought WWF Intercontinental champion Don Muraco to a no contest.

Ric Flair verses **Victor Jovica** for the NWA World heavyweight title at Ato Boldon, Couva Trinidad with 24,000 fans again at a near riot and Flair again appears to put a wrestler over for the NWA title in order to escape a Caribbean nation alive.

DragonKingKarl Note: Ric Flair, at least three times, let a Caribbean wrestling star appear to win the NWA World heavyweight title to avoid a riot or fan attack. Jack Veneno, Victor Jovica, and Carlos Colon all have "appeared" to win the NWA World title under these circumstances and many of the stories get confused with one another. You can read more about the original Jack Veneno win at our website WhenItWasCool.com in the *Ultimate History of Pro Wrestling Zone* under the year 1982.

02-09-1983: In Miami, FL in front of a crowd of 6,196 The Midnight Rider (Dusty Rhodes) defeated Ric Flair for the NWA World heavyweight title but had to give up the title when he refused to unmask. Results: Andre the Giant & Barry Windham defeated Kevin Sullivan & Jake Roberts... Mike Graham defeated Don Kent... Roddy Piper defeated Mr. NY and unmasked him as Chic Donovan... Rufus R. Jones & Ron Bass defeated Angelo Mosca & Leroy Brown by DQ... Charlie Cook defeated Cyclone Negro... Scott McGhee & Terry Allen defeated The Kangaroos (Don Kent & Johnny Heffernan) by DQ.

02-11-1983: A huge card was held in St. Louis, MO at the Checkerdome in front of 16,695 fans. It was shown on Japanese television and featured a PWF title change and a famous Ric Flair verses Bruiser Brody match. Results: Roger Kirby defeated Manny Fernandez... Bill Cody & Buzz Tyler & Rick Martel defeated

Crusher Ayala (Hercules Ayala) & Dewey Robertson & Kim Duk... Ken Patera defeated Ox Baker... Butch Reed defeated Bobby Duncum... Bob Orton, Jr. & Dick Murdoch defeated Bob Brown & Dick the Bruiser... Kerry Von Erich defeated Greg Valentine to retain the Missouri heavyweight title... NWA World champion Ric Flair went to a time limit draw with Bruiser Brody in a best 2 out of 3 falls match... Giant Baba defeated Harley Race to win the PWF heavyweight title.

WWF: Pittsburgh, PA: Civic Arena: Attendance: 10,000: Pete Sanchez pinned Charlie Fulton... SD Jones pinned Johnny Rodz... Salvatore Bellomo pinned Baron Mikel Scicluna... The Wild Samoans (Afa & Sika) defeated Eddie Gilbert & Curt Hennig... Big John Studd defeated Jules Strongbow... WWF champion Bob Backlund pinned WWF Intercontinental champion Don Muraco in a Texas Death Match... Ray Stevens defeated Pedro Morales via count-out... Rocky Johnson defeated Superstar Billy Graham via DQ... Jimmy Snuka pinned Buddy Rose... Chief Jay Strongbow fought Mr. Fuji to a DQ... Tony Garea pinned Swede Hanson.

02-12-1983: In Sarasota, FL Midnight Rider (Dusty Rhodes) defeated NWA World heavyweight champion Ric Flair but did not win the title, once again, due to the "refuse to unmask" stipulation.

AWA in Chicago, IL: Steve O battled Tom Lintz to a draw... Bobby Heenan beat Buck Zumhofe... Rick Martel beat Sgt. Rene Goulet by DQ... Wahoo McDaniel beat Bobby Duncum... Jerry Lawler beat Ken Patera... Hulk Hogan beat Jesse

Ventura by DQ... Greg Gagne & Jim Brunzell battled Sgt. Goulet & Sheik Jerry Blackwell to a no contest.

02-13-1983: NWA World heavyweight champion Ric Flair fought Andre the Giant to a double count out in Orlando, FL.

Hulk Hogan defeated Jesse Ventura and Greg Gagne & Jim Brunzell defeated Ken Patera & Bobby Duncum at the Civic Center, St. Paul, MN draws 16,000 fans.

02-14-1983: In Memphis, TN at the Mid-South Coliseum in front of 6,437: Kenya Condori pinned Bobby Fulton... Sweet Brown Sugar (Koko Ware) pinned Sabu (Coco Samoa)... Jesse Barr wrestled Dutch Mantel to a draw... Bobby Eaton pinned King Cobra... Bill Dundee beat Apocalypse (Mike Boyer) via forfeit... The Fabulous Ones (Steve Keirn & Stan Lane) beat U.S. tag team champions The Executioners via DQ... Bobby Eaton beat Bill Dundee via DQ... Sweet Brown Sugar (Koko Ware) pinned Jesse Barr... Terry Taylor beat Jerry Roberts (Jacques Rougeau) in a no DQ match to win the Southern title... Bobby Eaton beat Sweet Brown Sugar to win the vacant Mid-America title... AWA World champion Nick Bockwinkel pinned Jerry Lawler.

In West Palm Beach, FL: NWA World heavyweight champion Ric Flair defeated Barry Windham in a steel cage match.

02-15-1983: In Tampa, FL Terry Allen & Midnight Rider (Dusty Rhodes) defeated The Kangaroos (Don Kent & Johnny Heffernan) to win the Global tag team titles but Midnight Rider gave up the belt to Scott McGhee. Also, NWA World heavyweight champion Ric Flair defeated Scott McGhee.

02-16-1983: It appears that **Rocky Johnson** wins the WWF Intercontinental title from Don Muraco in Hamburg, PA but it was later changed to a DQ due to interference by Captain Lou Albano. The TV commentary left viewers in doubt as to whether or not they had seen a title change.

DragonKingKarl Note: Rocky Johnson was, as is famously known, the father of pro wrestling mega-star and action movie giant Dwayne "The Rock" Johnson.

02-17-1983: In Ocala, FL at the Jai Alai Fronton: NWA World heavyweight champion Ric Flair defeated Barry Windham.

02-18-1983: WWF in New York City, NY at Madison Square Garden. Results: Jose Estrada defeated Curt Hennig… Johnny Rodz defeated Baron Mikel Scicluna… Mr. Fuji defeated Tony Garea… Big John Studd defeated Jules Strongbow… Ray Stevens defeated Chief Jay Strongbow… WWF Intercontinental champion Don Muraco defeated WWF champion Bob Backlund by DQ… Rocky Johnson defeated Superstar Billy Graham managed by the Grand Wizard by count out… Andre the Giant & Jimmy Snuka defeated the Wild Samoans (Afa & Sika) managed by Captain Lou Albano… Eddie Gilbert defeated Charlie Fulton… Salvatore Bellomo defeated Swede Hanson… Pedro Morales defeated Buddy Rose.

02-19-1983: WWF in Philadelphia, PA at the Spectrum in front of 18,246 fans. Results: Jose Estrada defeated Curt Hennig… Johnny Rodz defeated Mac Rivera… Tony Garea defeated Charlie Fulton… Swede Hanson defeated SD Jones… Eddie Gilbert defeated Baron Mikel Scicluna… Big John Studd defeated

WWF champion Bob Backlund by countout... The Wild Samoans (Afa & Sika) defeated Chief Jay & Jules Strongbow... Andre the Giant & Rocky Johnson & Salvatore Bellomo & Jimmy Snuka & Pedro Morales defeated Mr. Fuji & Ray Stevens & Don Muraco & Buddy Rose & Superstar Billy Graham in a best 3 out of 5 falls match.

AWA in Rockford, IL saw Nick Bockwinkel defeat Hulk Hogan by DQ to retain the title.

02-20-1983: In Memphis, TN at the Mid-South Coliseum in front of 4,965 fans. Jerry Lawler defeated AWA World heavyweight champion Nick Bockwinkel by forfeit (Bockwinkel arrived late to the arena). As a substitute match Austin Idol defeated Jerry Lawler in a no DQ match... Sweet Brown Sugar (Koko Ware) defeated Bobby Eaton for the Mid-America title. Adrian Street & Jesse Barr beat The Fabulous Ones (Steve Keirn & Stan Lane) to win the Southern tag team titles. Keirn pinned Street, but the dazed referee declared the wrong winner.

In Toronto, Canada at Maple Leaf Gardens with a crowd of 13,798: Rudy Kay & Nick DeCarlo battled Private Jim Nelson (Later known as: Boris Zhukoff) & Tim Gerrard to a draw... Johnny Weaver defeated Bobby Bass... The Destroyer (Dick Beyer) defeated Terry Kay... Leo Burke battled Tony Parisi to a double count out... Salvatore Bellomo defeated Ray Stevens by DQ... Ricky Steamboat & Jay Youngblood defeated Sgt. Slaughter & Don Kernodle in a non-title Boot Camp match... NWA World heavyweight champion Ric Flair defeated Terry Funk.

02-24-1983: Ric Flair defends the NWA World heavyweight title in Auckland, New Zealand defeating Mark Lewin.

02-25-1983: NWA World heavyweight champion Ric Flair defeats Mark Lewin in New Plymouth, New Zealand.

AWA in St. Paul, MN: Brad Rheingans battled AWA World heavyweight champion Nick Bockwinkel to a draw… Hulk Hogan beat Mr. Saito & David Schultz… Greg Gagne & Jim Brunzell & Rick Martel beat Ken Patera & Crusher Blackwell & Sheik Adnon Al Kaissey… Blackjack Lanza beat Bobby Heenan by count out… Buck Zumhofe beat Steve Regal… Steve O battled Bill White to a draw.

02-26-1983: NWA World heavyweight champion Ric Flair defeats Mark Lewin in Christchurch, New Zealand.

02-27-1983: NWA World champion Ric Flair continues his tour of New Zealand against Mark Lewin this time wrestling him in Dunedin.

The Gillette Cup is held by WWC promotion with Carlos Colon winning at Hiram Bithorn Stadium, San Juan, Puerto Rico with 12,000 fans.

GCW at the Omni in Atlanta, GA: Ole Anderson & Buzz Sawyer battled Stan Hansen & Masked Superstar (Bill Eadie) to a draw… No DQ: Butch Reed defeated Ivan Koloff… Bruiser Brody battled Abdullah the Butcher to a draw… Paul Orndorff defeated The Assassin (Jody Hamilton)… Dick Murdoch defeated Iron Sheik… Brian Blair & Tito Santana & Ray Candy defeated The Moondogs (Rex &

Spot) & Super Destroyer (Scott Irwin)... Paul Orndorff defeated Joe Lightfoot... Bob Roop defeated Tom Prichard.

AWA in Denver, CO: Jerry Lawler beat Sgt. Rene Goulet... Rick Martel beat Bobby Heenan... Mad Dog Vachon & Verne Gagne beat Sheik Adnon Al Kaissey & Jerry Blackwell... Wahoo McDaniel battled Ken Patera to a no contest... Hulk Hogan beat Jesse Ventura by DQ in arm wrestling.

02-28-1983: NWA World champion Ric Flair faces Mark Lewin in Invercargill, New Zealand.

Southwest Wrestling (Joe Blanchard Promotions) in San Antonio, TX Bob Sweetan defeated Tully Blanchard for the Southwest heavyweight title.

March 1983

03-01-1983: At the Mid-South Coliseum in Memphis, TN in front of 4,573 fans Bobby Eaton defeated Sweet Brown Sugar (Koko Ware) in a loser-leave town match to win the Mid-America title.

03-03-1983: NWA World champion Ric Flair defeats Mark Lewin to retain the title in Auckland, New Zealand. There is a brawl after the match and Lewin leaves ringside with the belt.

WWF champion Bob Backlund defeated WWF Intercontinental champion Don Muraco in Monaca, PA.

AWA World champion Nick Bockwinkel defeated Hulk Hogan by DQ in Winnipeg, Manitoba Canada.

03-04-1983: NWA World heavyweight champion Ric Flair continues his tour of New Zealand. This time his opponent is promoter and wrestler Steve Rickard in Hamilton, New Zealand.

03-05-1983: WWF: San Diego, CA: 5,000: First WWF wrestling show in the Bay Area: Jack Armstrong fought the Great Yatsu to a draw… Blackjack Mulligan defeated Billy Anderson… Pat Patterson defeated Jerry Monti… Buddy Rose defeated Tony Garea… WWF Intercontinental champion Don Muraco defeated Jules Strongbow… Chief Jay Strongbow defeated Black Gordman… Pedro Morales defeated Superstar Billy Graham via DQ… Andre the Giant defeated Mr. Fuji & Alexis Smirnoff in a handicap match… WWF champion Bob Backlund defeated Ray Stevens… Andre the Giant won a 17-man battle royal.

NWA World heavyweight champion **Ric Flair** goes from one side of the world to the other. Tonight he wrestles against and defeats Denny Brown on Georgia Championship Wrestling in Atlanta, GA at the WTBS studios.

DragonKingKarl Note: While many wrestlers heavily exaggerate their wrestling schedules from the 1980s, Ric Flair didn't. Ric Flair's travel schedule as the National Wrestling Alliance (NWA) World heavyweight champion was insane. Often, he would be wrestling several thousand miles apart on adjoining days. This trip from New Zealand to Atlanta, GA is particularly notable.

03-06-1983: The Wild Samoans (Afa & Sika) managed by Captain Lou Albano defeated Jules & Chief Jay Strongbow to win the WWF tag team titles in Los Angeles, CA.

03-07-1983: In Memphis, TN: Mid-South Coliseum drawing 5,657: Jim Dalton beat Sabu (Coco Samoa) via DQ... Terry Taylor & Ricky Morton wrestled The Galaxians (Ken Wayne & Danny Davis) to a draw... Dutch Mantel pinned Jerry Roberts (Jacques Rougeau) in a loser-leave town match... Bill Dundee & Steve O beat The Sheepherders (Jonathan Boyd & Luke Williams) in a back alley street brawl match... Stagger Lee (Koko Ware) pinned Bobby Eaton to win the Mid-America title... Southern tag team champions The Fabulous Ones (Steve Keirn & Stan Lane) beat Adrian Street & Jesse Barr... Jerry Lawler pinned Austin Idol to win the CWA International Title.

Bob Armstrong defeated Jimmy Golden to win the NWA Southeastern title in Birmingham, AL in a Texas Death Match. Mr. Olympia (Jerry Stubbs) won a tournament to get a shot at NWA World heavyweight champion Ric Flair.

DragonKingKarl Note: Bob Armstrong was incredible during this time period as a heel. Bob Armstrong had turned heel in the fall of 1982 against Ron Fuller during Fuller's NWA World title match against Ric Flair in Mobile, AL. Bob Armstrong, the presumed friend of Ron Fuller at the time, had been appointed as special guest referee in the match and turned on Ron Fuller and helped Ric Flair "injure" his leg and put him out of wrestling for several months. Bob Armstrong grew a terrible mustache, as a forty-plus year old man in the south in 1983 he started wearing an earring, and despite the fact fans knew he was married and his children Scott and

Brad Armstrong were already wrestling, heel Bob Armstrong began openly bragging about having a relationship and getting lavish gifts from a woman called "Fannie Mae Titweiler". Bob Armstrong, always known as one of the best hometown hero babyfaces in pro wrestling turned out to also be an incredible heel.

03-08-1983: The Kangaroos (Don Kent & Johnny Heffernan) defeated Terry Allen & Scott McGhee to win the Global tag team titles in Tampa, FL.

AWA: Salt Lake City, UT: Attendance: 10,400: Baron Von Raschke defeated Bobby Heenan by count out… Fabulous Moolah defeated Sabrina… Jerry Lawler defeated John Tolos… Jesse Ventura defeated Hulk Hogan by DQ… Highfliers (Jim Brunzell & Greg Gagne) & Mad Dog Vachon defeated Sgt. Jacques Rene Goulet & Sheik Adnon El Kaissey & Jerry Blackwell.

03-11-1983: Chavo Guerrero defeated AWA World champion Nick Bockwinkel by DQ at the Sam Houston Coliseum in Houston, TX. Also on the show Tiger Conway, Jr. & Mr. Wrestling II (Johnny Walker) defeated Ted DiBiase & Matt Borne to win the Mid-South tag team titles.

JCP: Hampton, VA: Coliseum: Attendance: 5,000: NWA World heavyweight champion Ric Flair defeated Dory Funk, Jr… Roddy Piper defeated Dick Slater… Ricky Steamboat & Jay Youngblood won a tag team match against unknown opponents… Terri Shane & Joyce Grable won a tag team match against unknown opponents.

03-12-1983: A big show for Jim Crockett Promotions takes place at the Greensboro, NC Coliseum. Attendance: 15,547 sell-out with an estimated 3,000-5,000 fans turned away. Results: Jerry Brisco defeated Ken Timbs… Mike Rotundo defeated Rick Harris (Later known as: Black Bart)… Jim Nelson (Later known as: Boris Zhukov) & Johnny Weaver defeated Red Dog Lane & Gene Anderson… Roddy Piper defeated Dick Slater but did not win the Mid-Atlantic TV title as the time limit for the title portion of the match had expired… NWA World heavyweight champion Ric Flair battled NWA U.S. Champion Greg Valentine to a 60 minute time limit draw… Ricky Steamboat & Jay Youngblood defeated NWA World tag team champions Sgt. Slaughter & Don Kernodle in a no time limit, steel cage match to win the NWA World tag team titles.

WWF at an evening show in Landover, MD at the Capital Centre results: Eddie Gilbert & Tony Garea defeated Mr. Fuji & Swede Hanson… Pedro Holmes defeated Johnny Rodz… Ray Stevens defeated SD Jones… Rocky Johnson defeated Baron Mikel Scicluna… Pete Sanchez went to a draw with Jose Estrada… Big John Studd defeated Chief Jay Strongbow… Jimmy Snuka defeated Superstar Billy Graham in a Texas Death Match… Andre the Giant won a battle royal. Participants included: Big John Studd, Mr. Fuji, Rocky Johnson, Afa, Sika, SD Jones, Chief Jay Strongbow, Ray Stevens, Jules Strongbow, Swede Hanson, Pedro Morales, Tony Garea, Baron Mikel Scicluna, Salvatore Bellomo, Charlie Fulton, Eddie Gilbert, Jose Estrada, Pete Sanchez, and Johnny Rodz… WWF champion Bob Backlund defeated WWF Intercontinental champion Don Muraco in a Texas Death Match.

At a WWF afternoon show in Baltimore, MD Wild Samoan Sika suffers a broken hip in a tag team match and is replaced for a time by The Samoan 3 (Samula). On television the injury was never addressed and old matches of The Samoans played instead and they continued their run as WWF tag team champions. On the same show Big John Studd defeated WWF champion Bob Backlund by DQ

On Southeastern Championship Wrestling (SECW) from the Dothan, AL television studio the Mongolian Stomper turns heel on **Austin Idol** in an angle known as "The Cure for Idol-mania" where the Mongolian Stomper was a hired hitman for NWA World champion Ric Flair.

DragonKingKarl Note: 1983 was a red hot year for Ron Fuller's SECW promotion. The late 1982 heel turn of Bob Armstrong against Ron Fuller set up Armstrong to be a very entertaining character for 1983 and led to several interesting programs before turning back babyface in the fall. Austin Idol was very popular in the area and Mr. Olympia (Jerry Stubbs) was splitting time between Bill Watts' Mid-South and SECW and having a great year.

03-13-1983: AWA in St. Paul, MN: Steve Regal battled Buck Zumhofe to a draw... Curt Hennig beat Sgt. Rene Goulet... Brad Rheingans beat John Tolos... Sheik Adnan Al Kaissey & Jerry Blackwell beat Mad Dog Vachon & Baron Von Raschke... Hulk Hogan & Greg Gagne & Jim Brunzell beat Bobby Heenan & Ken Patera & Jesse Ventura... AWA World heavyweight champion Nick Bockwinkel beat Rick Martel.

03-14-1983: WCCW: Fort Worth, TX: Will Rogers Coliseum: Attendance 8,000: The largest crowd in Fort Worth wrestling history: King Kong Bundy defeats The Texan (Jake Roberts)… Little Coco defeats Billy The Kid… Jimmy Garvin defeats Brian Adias… Iceman Parsons defeats Killer Karl Krupp… Ken Mantell defeats Bill Irwin… The Great Kabuki defeats Tola Yatsu (Yoshiaki Yatsu) by DQ… World Class World Six Man Tag Team champions The Fabulous Freebirds (Buddy Roberts & Michael Hayes & Terry Gordy) defeat The Von Erichs (David Von Erich & Kerry Von Erich & Kevin Von Erich)

03-17-1983: Frank Dusek defeated Barry Windham to win the Southern (FL) heavyweight title on TV in Tampa, FL.

03-18-1983: WWF: Steubenville, OH: St. Johns Arena: Attendance: 6,500: Jose Estrada pinned Bill Dixon… Salvatore Bellomo pinned Mac Rivera… Jimmy Snuka pinned Ray Stevens… Superstar Billy Graham pinned Pete Sanchez… Baron Mikel Scicluna pinned Joe Abby… Rocky Johnson & Andre the Giant defeated Wild Samoan Afa & Capt. Lou Albano via count-out.

WWF: Boston, MA: Boston Garden: Attendance: 16,174: Jose Estrada defeated Pete Doherty… Pete Sanchez defeated Baron Mikel Scicluna… Tony Garea defeated Fred Marsino… Chief Jay Strongbow defeated Lou Albano… Iron Mike Sharpe defeated SD Jones… WWF champion Bob Backlund defeated Don Muraco… Rocky Johnson defeated Superstar Billy Graham… Andre the Giant defeated Big John Studd… Ray Stevens defeated Jules Strongbow… Johnny Rodz defeated The Samoan 3 (Samu).

03-19-1983: WWF: Philadelphia, PA: Spectrum: Ray Stevens battled Jules Strongbow to a double count out… Bob Backlund & Andre the Giant & Jimmy Snuka defeated Big John Studd & Samoan Afa & Lou Albano… SD Jones defeated Baron Mikel Scicluna… Jose Estrada defeated Pete Sanchez… Don Muraco defeated Rocky Johnson.

03-20-1983: WWF in New York City, NY at Madison Square Garden with an attendance of 26,109. Results: Mac Rivera defeated Baron Mikel Scicluna… Tony Garea defeated Johnny Rodz… SD Jones defeated Jose Estrada… Pancho Boy & Sonny Boy Hayes defeated Farmer Pete & Butch Cassidy… Superstar Billy Graham, managed by the Grand Wizard, defeated Jules Strongbow… Salvatore Bellomo battled Ray Stevens to a double count out… WWF champion Bob Backlund defeated WWF Intercontinental champion Don Muraco in a Texas Death Match… Andre the Giant & Rocky Johnson & Jimmy Snuka defeated Big John Studd & Afa & Captain Lou Albano in a best 3 out of 5 falls match.

At the Omni in Atlanta, GA Killer Tim Brooks defeated Paul Orndorff to win the NWA National heavyweight title which will be sold to Larry Zbyszko… Tommy Rich defeated Larry Zbyszko… Canadian Lumberjack Match: Stan Hansen & Masked Superstar (Bill Eadie) defeated Ole Anderson & Buzz Sawyer… Dick Murdoch defeated Ivan Koloff by DQ… Tony Atlas defeated Iron Sheik… Brad Armstrong & Ray Candy defeated Paul Ellering & Moondog Rex… Brett Sawyer battled Joe Lightfoot to a draw… Brian Blair defeated Chick Donovan.

AWA in Denver, CO: Hulk Hogan battled Jesse Ventura to a no contest… Jerry Lawler beat Ken Patera… Brad Rheingans beat John Tolos… Greg Gagne & Jim

Brunzell beat Sheik Adnon Al Kaissey & Jerry Blackwell... AWA World heavyweight champion Nick Bockwinkel beat Rick Martel.

03-21-1983: Mid-South North American title tournament in New Orleans, LA: Round 1: Mr. Olympia (Jerry Stubbs) defeated Marty Lunde (Later known as: Arn Anderson)... Mr. Wrestling II (Johnny Walker) defeated Bill Irwin... Butch Reed defeated Super Destroyer (Scott Irwin)... Tito Santana defeated Matt Borne. Round 2: Mr. Wrestling II (Johnny Walker) battled Kamala to a double DQ... Butch Reed defeated Jim Duggan... Kendo Nagasaki defeated Tito Santana by count out... Junkyard Dog defeated Ted DiBiase. Round 3: Mr. Olympia defeated Butch Reed... Junkyard Dog defeated Kendo Nagasaki. Finals: Mr. Olympia defeated Junkyard Dog to win the vacant North American title.

In Memphis, TN: Mid-South Coliseum drawing 6,162: Sonny King pinned Carl Fergie... Duke Myers pinned Bobby Fulton... Steve O pinned Jonathon Boyd... **The Rock-n-Roll Express (Ricky Morton & Robert Gibson)** beat The Galaxians (Ken Wayne & Danny Davis) via DQ.. The Sheepherders (Jonathan Boyd & Luke Williams) & Adrian Street & Jesse Barr beat The Fabulous Ones (Steve Keirn & Stan Lane) & Steve O & Dutch Mantel... Bill Dundee pinned Terry Taylor to win the Southern title... Stagger Lee (Koko Ware) & Jerry Lawler & Andre The Giant beat Porkchop Cash & Mad Dog & Bobby Eaton.

DragonKingKarl Note: One of the greatest tag teams in pro wrestling history, the Rock & Roll Express, is formed when Ricky Morton, who had been wrestling as an undercard babyface in Memphis, is teamed up with Robert Gibson who had been a junior heavyweight champion in Southeastern Wrestling. Robert Gibson's older brother Rick Gibson was a well known star in the area. The Rock & Roll Express were created to ride on the popularity of the babyface team of The Fabulous Ones (Steve Keirn & Stan Lane) as a way of having a hot babyface tag team on alternate shows or in the area when The Fabulous Ones were wrestling elsewhere. While the Rock & Roll Express were successful in Memphis, their real rise to fame would begin later in the year when they migrated, along with other talent, from Memphis to Bill Watts' Mid-South wrestling where they would have a legendary feud with the Midnight Express (Dennis Condrey & Bobby Eaton managed by Jim Cornette).

03-23-1983: Scott McGhee defeated Johnny Heffernan in Tampa, FL on TV to win the vacant Florida title.

03-24-1983: Hulk Hogan defeated AWA World heavyweight champion Nick Bockwinkel by DQ with Wahoo McDaniel as special referee in Winnipeg, Canada.

03-25-1983: The All-Japan Pro Wrestling Champion Carnival Tournament begins and scheduled for the tour are: Ric Flair, Nick Bockwinkel, Bruiser Brody, Stan Hansen, Harley Race, Dory Funk, Jr., Terry Funk, Mil Mascaras, Jerry Lawler, Ted DiBiase, Paul Orndorff, Ivan Koloff, Alexis Smirnoff, Chavo Guerrero, Hector Guerrero, David Von Erich, Kerry Von Erich, Jimmy Snuka, Dynamite Kid, Dos Caras, Ron Bass, Dick Slater, Terry Gordy, and Michael Hayes. (Per Dave Meltzer's *Wrestling Observer Newsletter* 03-1983 issue)

03-26-1983: In Jacksonville, FL Barry Windham defeated Angelo Mosca to win the Canadian title.

WWF: Boston, MA: Boston Garden: Attendance 16,147 (sellout): Jose Estrada defeats Pete Doherty… Tony Garea defeats Fred Marzino… Pete Sanchez defeats Baron Mikel Scicluna… Chief Jay Strongbow defeats Captain Lou Albano… Iron Mike Sharpe defeats SD Jones… Jimmy Snuka defeats Afa… WWF champion Bob Backlund defeats WWF Intercontinental champion Don Muraco in a Texas Death match… Rocky Johnson defeats Superstar Billy Graham… Andre the Giant defeats Big John Studd by Count Out… Ray Stevens defeats Jules Strongbow… Johnny Rodz defeats Samula by DQ.

03-27-1983: Roddy Piper defeated Mid-Atlantic TV champion Dick Slater in Asheville, NC at the Civic Center to win the title.

In Toronto, Canada at the Maple Leaf Gardens Jim Nelson (Later known as: Boris Zhukov) defeated Terry Kay to win the Canadian TV title. On the same show NWA World heavyweight champion Ric Flair defeated Roddy Piper to retain the title… NWA World team champions Ricky Steamboat & Jay Youngblood defeat Don Kernodle & Sgt. Slaughter in a steel cage match.

03-28-1983: In Ft. Worth, TX at the Civic Center Iceman King Parsons defeated Tola Yatsu (Yoshiaki Yatsu) for the World Class TV title.

In Green Bay, WI Wahoo McDaniel defeated AWA World heavyweight champion Nick Bockwinkel by DQ.

In San Antonio, TX: Tully Blanchard & Gino Hernandez defeated The Grapplers (Len Denton & Tony Anthony) for the Southwest tag team titles. Tully hit Gino with the belt and it was declared vacant.

03-29-1983: Sgt. Slaughter returns to the WWF defeating Barry Hart (Barry Horowitz).

03-30-1983: In Miami Beach, FL Terry Allen & Scott McGhee defeated The Kangaroos (Don Kent & Johnny Heffernan) to win the Global tag team titles.

April 1983

04-03-1983: GCW at the Omni in Atlanta, GA: NWA World heavyweight champion Ric Flair defeated Tony Atlas by DQ... Larry Zbyszko defeated Tommy Rich... Dick Murdoch & Dusty Rhodes defeated Iron Sheik & Ivan Koloff... Masked Superstar (Bill Eadie) defeated Buzz Sawyer by DQ... Matt Borne & Arn Anderson defeated Brian Blair & Tito Santana... Killer Brooks defeated Brett Wayne... Paul Ellering defeated Joe Lightfoot.

In San Antonio, TX: The Grapplers (Len Denton & Tony Anthony) won the Southwest tag team titles beating Mando Guerrero & Bob Sweetan in the finals of a tournament.

New Japan Pro Wrestling: in Tokyo, Japan: Sumo Hall: Buddy Rose & Ed Leslie beat Osamu Kido & Ryuma Go... Paul Orndorff beat Animal Hamaguchi... Masa Saito & Killer Khan beat Seiji Sakaguchi & Kengo Kimura... Kuniaki Kobayashi battled Dynamite Kid to a double count out. This match was for the vacant WWF Junior Heavyweight title... Riki Choshu beat Tatsumi Fujinami to win the WWF International title... Antonio Inoki pinned Rusher Kimura.

04-04-1983: In Memphis, TN: Mid-South Coliseum drawing 6.716: Carl Fergie beat Sonny King via DQ… Duke Myers pinned Bobby Fulton… Bobby Eaton drew The Ace of Spades (Tommy Gilbert)… Porkchop Cash & Dream Machine (Troy Graham) beat Dutch Mantel & Steve O… Mid-America champion Stagger Lee (Koko Ware) beat Giant Frazier in a mask & title vs. $1,000 match… **The Galaxians (Ken Wayne & Danny Davis)** beat The Rock-n-Roll Express (Ricky Morton & Robert Gibson) in a match where the Galaxians masks were at stake… Terry Taylor beat Southern champion Bill Dundee via DQ in a match with two referees… The Moondogs (Rex & Spot) beat The Fabulous Ones (Steve Keirn & Stan Lane) to win the Southern tag team titles… AWA World champion Nick Bockwinkel beat Jerry Lawler via DQ.

DragonKingKarl Note: The Galaxians (Ken Wayne & Danny Davis) were better known as The Nightmares in both Memphis and later in SECW/Continental wrestling. They occasionally switched to this Galaxian gimmick as well, using it here in Memphis and later as an undercard tag team in NWA/WCW.

04-07-1983: Jerry Lawler defeated AWA World heavyweight champion Nick Bockwinkel by DQ in Lexington, KY.

04-08-1983: AWA in Denver, CO: Jerry Blackwell beat Brad Rheingans… Rick Martel beat Sheik Adnan Al Kaissey… Baron Von Raschke & Hulk Hogan & Mad Dog Vachon beat Ken Patera & Jesse Ventura & Bobby Heenan… AWA World heavyweight champion Nick Bockwinkel beat Wahoo McDaniel.

04-09-1983: Dusty Rhodes & Dick Murdoch announce on Georgia Championship Wrestling television that they are reforming the Texas Outlaws tag team to challenge Iron Sheik & Ivan Koloff.

WWF: Baltimore, MD; Civic Center: Attendance: 12,040: Bob Bradley defeated Mac Rivera... Pete Sanchez defeated Jose Estrada... Salvatore Bellomo defeated Charlie Fulton... Johnny Rodz defeated Baron Mikel Scicluna... Mr. Fuji defeated SD Jones... Little Poncho & Butch Cassidy defeated Tiger Jackson & Sonny Boy Hayes... Rocky Johnson pinned Ray Stevens... WWF Intercontinental champion Don Muraco defeated Pedro Morales via DQ... Jimmy Snuka pinned Superstar Billy Graham... WWF champion Bob Backlund pinned Big John Studd in a Texas Death match. Swede Hanson was the guest referee.

04-10-1983: Johnny Weaver defeated Leo Burke to win the North American title at the Toronto, Canada Maple Leaf Gardens. On the same show NWA World heavyweight champion Ric Flair defeated Roddy Piper by DQ.

04-11-1983: In Memphis, TN: Mid-South Coliseum drawing 6,366: Duke Myers beat Bobby Fulton... Porkchop Cash & Dream Machine (Troy Graham) beat Steve O & Carl Fergie... The Galaxians (Ken Wayne & Danny Davis) beat The Rock-n-Roll Express (Ricky Morton & Robert Gibson) in a Texas tornado match where the Galaxians masks were at stake... Southern champion Bill Dundee battled Dutch Mantel to a double count out... Stagger Lee (Koko Ware) & Terry Taylor beat Giant Frazier (Later known as Uncle Elmer in the WWF) & Jimmy Hart & Bobby Eaton in a handicap hair vs. hair match. Giant Stan Frazier had his head shaved... Southern tag team champions The Moondogs (Rex & Spot) beat

The Fabulous Ones (Steve Keirn & Stan Lane)... Jerry Lawler beat AWA World champion Nick Bockwinkel via DQ in a match where there was no referee in the ring.

Bob Armstrong defeated Ken Lucas to win the NWA Southeastern title in Birmingham, AL.

In West Palm Beach, FL: NWA World heavyweight champion Ric Flair defeated Dusty Rhodes by DQ.

04-12-1983: Jerry Lawler defeated AWA World heavyweight champion Nick Bockwinkel by DQ in Louisville, KY.

In Tampa, FL at the Fort Hesterly Armory: NWA World heavyweight champion Ric Flair defeated Big Daddy (Steve DiBlasio) by DQ.

04-13-1983: On a Mid-South television taping at the Irish McNeill's Boys Club in Shreveport, LA Ted DiBiase & Mr. Olympia (Jerry Stubbs) defeated Mr. Wrestling II (Johnny Walker) & Tiger Conway, Jr. to win the Mid-South tag team titles.

In Miami Beach, FL at the Convention Center: Attendance: 6,271: NWA World heavyweight champion Ric Flair defeated Barry Windham... Dusty Rhodes & Big Daddy (Steve DiBlasio) & Blackjack Mulligan defeated Angelo Mosca & Kevin Sullivan & Purple Haze (Mark Lewin)... Adrian Street defeated Scott McGhee to win the Florida title... Terry Allen (Later known as: Magnum TA) & Brad Armstrong defeated The Kangaroos (Johnny Heffernan & Don Kent) to win the Global tag team titles... Charlie Cook defeated Frank Dusek by DQ.

04-15-1983: WWF: Pittsburgh, PA: Civic Arena: Attention: 18,000: Eddie Gilbert pinned Rocky Cole… Tony Garea pinned Baron Mikel Scicluna… Women's Champion the Fabulous Moolah & Donna Christanello defeated Kandi Malloy & Penny Mitchell… Rocky Johnson defeated WWF Intercontinental champion Don Muraco via DQ… Mr. Fuji defeated Pedro Morales via count-out… Salvatore Bellomo defeated Superstar Billy Graham via count-out… Bob Backlund & Jimmy Snuka & Andre the Giant defeated Big John Studd & Afa & Samula.

04-16-1983: Roddy Piper defeated Greg Valentine to win the NWA U.S. title in Greensboro, NC at the Coliseum.

In another disputed Dusty Rhodes title reversal, The Midnight Rider (Dusty Rhodes) appears to have again defeated NWA World heavyweight champion Ric Flair for the title in St. Petersburg, FL at the Bayfront Center but the decision was reversed due to an official referee not counting the pinfall.

Mid-South Wrestling holds a show at the Superdome in New Orleans, LA: Attendance: 21,400: Junkyard Dog defeated Mr. Olympia (Jerry Stubbs) to win the North American title in a steel cage match… David & Kerry Von Erich defeated Terry Gordy & Buddy Roberts… Andre the Giant defeated Kamala… Butch Reed defeated Kendo Nagasaki… Mr. Olympia & Ted DiBiase defeated Mr. Wrestling II (Johnny Walker) & Tiger Conway, Jr… Chavo Guerrero defeated Bill Irwin… Art Crews defeated Kelly Kiniski… King Kong Bundy defeated Tim Horner.

In Austin, TX: Adrian Adonis defeated Bob Sweetan to win the Southwest heavyweight title.

AWA in Chicago, IL: Brad Rheingans beat Rocky Stone... Rick Martel beat John Tolos...Joyce Grable & Wendi Richter beat Judy Martin & Velvet McIntyre... Wahoo McDaniel beat Sheik Adnan Al Kaissey... Mad Dog Vachon beat Jerry Blackwell by DQ... Hulk Hogan & Greg Gagne & Jim Brunzell beat Ken Patera & Jesse Ventura & Bobby Heenan... AWA World heavyweight champion Nick Bockwinkel beat Jerry Lawler.

WWF: Boston, MA: Boston Garden: Attendance 13,233: Johnny Rodz defeats Charlie Fulton... Salvatore Bellomo defeats Jose Estrada... Eddie Gilbert & Tony Garea defeat Mr. Fuji & Swede Hanson... Chief Jay Strongbow defeats Superstar Billy Graham... WWF champion Bob Backlund defeats Big John Studd... Iron Mike Sharpe defeats Jules Strongbow... Rocky Johnson defeats WWF Intercontinental Title Match Don Muraco by Count Out... Ray Stevens defeats SD Jones... Jimmy Snuka & Pedro Morales defeat Afa & Samula.

04-17-1983: GCW at the Omni in Atlanta, GA: In a Bullrope & Chain Match: Texas Outlaws (Dick Murdoch & Dusty Rhodes) defeated Ivan Koloff & Iron Sheik... Larry Zbyszko defeated Tommy Rich... Tony Atlas defeated Buzz Sawyer by DQ... Matt Borne & Arn Anderson defeated Ray Candy & Joe Lightfoot... Ronnie Garvin defeated Killer Brooks... Paul Ellering defeated Tito Santana... Brett Wayne defeated Chick Donovan... Brian Blair defeated Pat Rose.

In Orlando, FL: Barry Windham battled NWA World heavyweight champion Ric Flair to a draw.

04-18-1983: In Memphis, TN: Mid-South Coliseum drawing 5,468: The Ace of Spades (Tommy Gilbert) drew Carl Fergie... Terry Taylor & Steve O beat Dream Machine (Troy Graham) & Porkchop Cash via DQ... Mid-America champion Stagger Lee (Koko Ware) beat Bobby Eaton via DQ in a mask & title vs. $1,500 match... The Rock & Roll Express (Rocky Morton & Robert Gibson) beat Galaxian Alpha (Danny Davis) & Jim Cornette in a match where the Express' hair was at stake... CWA International champion Jerry Lawler pinned Duke Meyers... Jerry Lawler beat Jimmy Hart & Jim Cornette in a handicap match... Southern champion Bill Dundee beat Dutch Mantel.

04-21-1983: New Japan Pro Wrestling Wrestling: in Tokyo, Japan: Sumo Hall drawing 14,000: Shown April 22, 1983 on TV: Animal Hamaguchi beat Osamu Kido... Seiji Sakaguchi & Kengo Kimura beat Isamu Teranishi & Rusher Kimura... Kuniaki Kobayashi beat Caswell Martin... Killer Khan beat Ed Leslie (Later known as Brutus Beefcake)... Akira Maeda pinned Paul Orndorff... Tiger Mask battled Dynamite Kid (Satoru Sayama) to a double count out... Riki Choshu beat Tatsumi Fujinami via countout... Antonio Inoki beat Masa Saito via submission in a loser-leaves-town match.

04-24-1983: JCP: Charlotte, NC: Coliseum: Attendance: 5,459: Ricky Harris (Later known as Black Bart) defeated Keith Larsen... Johnny Weaver defeated Masa Fuchi... Magic Dragon defeated Jim Nelson... Jake Roberts defeated Sweet Brown Sugar (Skip Young)... Jimmy Valiant defeated Great Kabuki... NWA US champion Roddy Piper fought NWA TV champion Dick Slater to a 15-minute time-limit draw... Sgt. Slaughter & Don Kernodle defeated NWA World tag team champions Ricky Steamboat & Jay Youngblood via disqualification... Greg Valentine defeated NWA World champion Ric Flair via disqualification.

AWA has a historically important Super Sunday show in St. Paul, MN: Attendance: 28,300, where it appeared that **Hulk Hogan** won the AWA World heavyweight title from champion Nick Bockwinkel but was ultimately ruled a DQ win. The other results on this show were: Verne Gagne & Mad Dog Vachon defeated Jerry Blackwell & Sheik Adnan... Ken Patera & Jesse Ventura & Blackjack Lanza defeated Greg Gagne & Jim Brunzell & Rick Martel... Jerry Lawler defeated John Tolos... Wahoo McDaniel defeated Ed Boulder (AKA: Brutus Beefcake)... Brad Rheingans defeated Tom Stone... Joyce Grable & Wendi Richter defeated Judy Martin & Velvet McIntyre.

DragonKingKarl Note: The *Saga of Hulk Hogan as the AWA World Champion* is a podcast special I did at *When It Was Cool Wrestling* detailing the myth and reality surrounding the question "Was Hulk Hogan actually ever AWA World champion"? There were actually multiple occasions where Hulk Hogan appeared to have won the AWA World title from Nick Bockwinkel, though *Super Sunday* is probably the most famous. Never-the-less, in people's memories, the multiple "wins the AWA World title" belief is really a mis-remembering of these different angles.

04-25-1983: WWF in New York City, NY at Madison Square Garden. Results: Eddie Gilbert defeated Jose Estrada... Salvatore Bellomo defeated Baron Mikel Scicluna... Mr. Fuji defeated SD Jones... Iron Mike Sharpe defeated Johnny Rodz... Pedro Morales defeated Swede Hanson... Ray Stevens defeated Tony Garea... Jimmy Snuka defeated Superstar Billy Graham (Graham's last match at

MSG for the next four years)… Rocky Johnson defeated WWF Intercontinental champion Don Muraco by count out… WWF World tag team champions Afa & Samula (substituting for Sika) defeated Chief Jay & Jules Strongbow… Andre the Giant defeated Big John Studd by countout… WWF champion Bob Backlund defeated Ivan Koloff.

At the Mid-South Coliseum in Memphis, TN in front of 4,667 fans The Fabulous Ones (Steve Keirn & Stan Lane) defeated The Moondogs (Rex & Spot) to win the held up Southern tag team titles.

04-28-1983: Iron Sheik defeated Ronnie Garvin for the NWA National TV title at the Omni in Atlanta, GA.

04-29-1983: David Shultz defeated AWA World champion Nick Bockwinkel by DQ in Calgary, Canada.

04-30-1983: Ron Bass defeated Frank Dusek for the Southern (FL) title in Ft. Myers, FL.

May 1983

05-01-1983: Greg Valentine defeated NWA U.S. champion Roddy Piper to win the title in Greensboro, NC.

GCW at the Omni in Atlanta, GA Tony Atlas defeated NWA World heavyweight champion Ric Flair by DQ… Tommy Rich & Paul Orndorff defeated Killer Brooks & Larry Zbyszko… Dick Murdoch defeated Buzz Sawyer by count out… Ronnie

Garvin defeated Iron Sheik... Matt Borne & Arn Anderson defeated Tito Santana & Brian Blair... Ray Candy defeated Chick Donovan... Bob Roop defeated Joe Lightfoot.

UWA Mexico: in Mexico City, Mexico: El Toreo drawing 25,000: Abdullah Tamba & Cuchillo & Escorpion I beat George Takano & Junji Hirata & Masa Saito... Irma Aguilar & Irma Gonzalez beat La Monster & Lola Gonzalez... Dory Dixon & Rayo de Jalisco beat Kahoz & Zandokan I... El Signo & Negro Navarro & El Texano beat Enrique Vera & Mano Negra & Villano III... Tatsumi Fujinami beat El Canek to win the UWA Heavyweight title.

05-02-1983: WWF champion Bob Backlund defeated WWF Intercontinental champion Don Muraco in Ogdensburg, NY.

A big show at the Mid-South Coliseum in Memphis, TN sees the return of Andy Kaufman to the ring to team up with the Colossus of Death (Duke Myers in a rubber mask) in front of a crowd of 9,194. Results: Jerry Lawler defeated The Colossus of Death & Andy Kauffman in a handicap match... Carl Fergie defeated Sonny King... Terry Taylor defeated the Ace of Spades (Tommy Gilbert)... Steve O defeated The Galaxian (Ken Wayne)... Stagger Lee (Koko Ware) & Mad Dog & Rock & Roll Express (Ricky Morton & Robert Gibson) defeated Bobby Eaton & Lone Ranger (Stan Frazier) & the Bruise Brothers (Porkchop Cash & Dream Machine) managed by Jimmy Hart... Bill Dundee defeated Dutch Mantel in a bullwhip match... The Moondogs (Rex & Spot) defeated The Fabulous Ones (Steve Keirn & Stan Lane) in a stretcher match.

05-03-1983: Rick Martel defeated AWA World heavyweight champion Nick Bockwinkel by DQ in Salt Lake City, UT.

Bret Hart defeated Leo Burke to win the Stampede North American title in Regina, Canada.

05-05-1983: Jerry Lawler defeated AWA World heavyweight champion Nick Bockwinkel by DQ in Lexington, KY.

05-07-1983: Southwest Wrestling (Joe Blanchard Promotion) in San Antonio, TX The Sheepherders (Luke Williams & Butch Miller) defeated The Grapplers (Len Denton & Tony Anthony) to win the Southwest tag team titles.

05-08-1983: Jack & Jerry Brisco win a tag team tournament for Jim Crockett Promotions in Savannah, GA to earn a shot at the NWA World tag team titles. In the tournament they defeated One Man Gang & Kelly Kiniski, Great Kabuki & Magic Dragon, and Jake Roberts & Dory Funk Jr.

05-09-1983: In Memphis, TN: Mid-South Coliseum drawing 7,618: The Ace of Spades (Tommy Gilbert) wrestled King Cobra to a draw… Porkchop Cash & Dream Machine (Troy Graham) beat Carl Fergie & Bobby Fulton… Steve O & Terry Taylor beat The Galaxians (Ken Wayne & Danny Davis)… The Rock-n-Roll Express (Ricky Morton & Robert Gibson) beat The Grapplers (Len Denton & Tony Anthony) via forfeit… Bobby Eaton & The Lone Ranger (Stan Frazier) beat Stagger Lee (Koko Ware) & Mad Dog… Jerry Lawler pinned The Colossus of Death (Duke Myers)… Jackie Fargo & Stan Lane beat The Moondogs (Rex &

Spot) in a stretcher match... Dutch Mantel beat Bill Dundee in a hair vs. title match to win the Southern title.

05-10-1983: Sgt. Slaughter interferes with WWF champion Bob Backlund's Harvard Step Test during a TV taping in Allentown, PA. Following this TV taping **Eddie Gilbert** was seriously injured in a car accident breaking his neck. Also following the show **Jimmy Snuka's** girlfriend Nancy Argentino is found dead in their hotel room. Over 30 years later Snuka is charged in her death in the case though he dies before he can go to trial. At the time the death was ruled an accident.

Promoter **Frank Tunney** died at the age of 70.

FA Cup Final Day Wrestling Special 1983 in Basildon, UK: Shown May 21, 1983 on ITV: Big Daddy & Kid Chocolate beat The Masked Marauders in three falls.

DragonKingKarl Note: On just about any other day in pro wrestling history, the story of young up-and-coming second generation wrestler Eddie Gilbert breaking his neck in a car accident would have been the top story. However, on May 10, 1983 there was a lot going on of historical importance. Long time Toronto wrestling promoter Frank Tunney passed away at the age of 70 in his sleep while on a trip to Hong Kong. But the biggest story of the day was the death of Nancy Argentino, the 23 year old girlfriend of WWF star Jimmy "Superfly" Snuka. Jimmy Snuka had already, earlier in the year, had a run-in with the law that resulted in his arrest and a significant amount of publicity in the newspapers as Jimmy Snuka, allegedly, bit one of the police dogs sent to arrest him following a disturbance with Nancy Argentino. Jimmy Snuka had gone to wrestle with Nancy Argentino left in his hotel room. Snuka returned after wrestling and found Argentino unresponsive and, ultimately, she was declared to be deceased. Jimmy Snuka was interviewed by police at the time with Vince McMahon (the "Junior" Vincent K. McMahon) supposedly assisting him during his interactions with investigators. There have long been allegations of ineptitude or disinterest at best and outright corruption at worst in the Nancy Argentino investigation. In 1983, the investigation largely went unprosecuted with law enforcement essentially accepting the story that Nancy Argentino slipped and fell down at a rest area along the highway, hit her head, and died later. In 2012, almost thirty years later, Jimmy Snuka released a biography titled: *Superfly: The Jimmy Snuka Story* written with author Jon Chattman, where Jimmy Snuka retales the story. Outraged by this, many people began reviving the story, most prominently journalist/author Irvin Muchnick who independently investigated and released a book called: *Justice Denied: The Untold Story of Nancy Argentino's Death in Jimmy Snuka's Motel Room*. This time, due to pressure from this newly found spotlight on Nancy Argentino's death, investigators had Jimmy Snuka arrested in 2015 and charged with Third Degree Murder and Involuntary Manslaughter, to which he pleaded not-guilty. Before the story could play out in the courts, however, an aged and sick Jimmy Snuka died at the age of 73 on January 15, 2017 without ultimate resolution via the court system.

05-13-1983: WWF: Pittsburgh, PA: Civic Arena: Attendance: 14,000: Mike Skully defeated Baron Mikel Scicluna via DQ… Ray Stevens fought Tony Garea to a draw… Rocky Johnson defeated WWF Intercontinental champion Don Muraco in a Texas Death Match... Jimmy Snuka pinned Mr. Fuji... Johnny DeFazio pinned Bill Dixon... Swede Hanson pinned Barry Hart (Barry Horowitz) ... WWF champion Bob Backlund defeated Ivan Koloff.

05-14-1983: WWF: Boston, MA: Boston Garden: Attendance 10,900: Mac Rivera defeats Fred Marzino... Pete Sanchez defeats Pete Doherty... SD Jones defeats Jose Estrada... Tony Garea defeats Ray Stevens by DQ... Mr. Fuji defeats Swede Hanson... Jimmy Snuka defeats Samula... Chief Jay Strongbow defeats Iron Mike Sharpe by DQ... WWF champion Bob Backlund defeats Ivan Koloff... Salvatore Bellomo defeats Johnny Rodz... WWF Intercontinental champion Don Muraco defeats Rocky Johnson in a Hawaiian Death match.

05-15-1983: GCW at the Omni in Atlanta, GA: Tony Atlas defeated Killer Brooks by DQ... Paul Orndorff defeated Larry Zbyszko... Brian Blair & Stan Hansen & Dick Murdoch battled Paul Ellering & Iron Sheik & Killer Brooks to a double DQ... Tommy Rich & Ray Candy defeated Matt Borne & Arn Anderson... Ronnie Garvin defeated Bob Roop... Brian Blair defeated Chick Donovan... Brett Wayne defeated Joe Lightfoot.

05-16-1983: Austin Idol defeated the Mongolian Stomper in a loser leave town match for Southeastern Wrestling in Birmingham, AL in a steel cage match. The Mongolian Stomper (Archie Gouldie), however, takes a page from Dusty Rhodes' booking in Florida, and soon returns under a mask as "The Midnight Stallion" and will, eventually, turn babyface.

At the Mid-South Coliseum in Memphis, TN in front of a crowd of 4,803 fans Duke Myers & Bobby Eaton defeated The Fabulous Ones (Steve Keirn & Stan Lane) for the Southern tag team titles. Also on the card: Ken Patera defeated Jerry Lawler for the International title. Bill Dundee defeated Dutch Mantel in a scaffold match to win the Southern title.

05-20-1983: A show featuring multiple world champions is held in Houston, TX. WWF champion Bob Backlund defeated Wild Samoan Afa… Junkyard Dog & Mr. Wrestling II (Johnny Walker) defeated King Kong Bundy & Mr. Olympia (Jerry Stubbs)… AWA World champion Nick Bockwinkel defeated Dusty Rhodes… Masked Superstar (Bill Eadie) & Super Destroyer (Scott Irwin) defeated Tito Santana & Mil Mascaras… Hacksaw Duggan defeated Kendo Nagasaki… Butch Reed defeated Rip Rogers… Gran Marcus defeated Johnny Rich.

05-21-1983: Mr. Gulf Coast defeats NWA World heavyweight champion Ric Flair by DQ on Southeastern Championship Wrestling television from Dothan, AL. Mr. Gulf Coast unmasks himself as Austin Idol.

AWA World champion Nick Bockwinkel battled Jerry Lawler to a no contest in Chicago, IL.

WWF: Baltimore, MD: Civic Center: Attendance: 8,000: Salvatore Bellomo defeated Bob Bradley… Susan Starr & Princess Victoria defeated Leilani Kai & Fabulous Moolah… Mac Rivera defeated Frank Williams… Swede Hanson defeated Fred Marzino… Samula defeated Tony Colon… Baron Mikel Scicluna defeated Rocky Cole… Afa defeated Jules Strongbow… Sika defeated Israel

Matia... Salvatore Bellomo won an 18-man $10,000 battle royal... WWF champion Bob Backlund defeated Ivan Koloff.

Southwest Wrestling (**Joe Blanchard**) Houston, TX: Adrian Adonis defeated Bob Orton, Jr. in the finals of a tournament for an "undisputed" World heavyweight title which would only be defended in the Southwest area. The belt was a close replica of the NWA "10 pounds of gold" domed globe title belt. The title only lasts until September.

DragonKingKarl Note: I have recently been going through every 1983 issue of Dave Meltzer's incredible *Wrestling Observer Newsletter* and following an interesting sub-plot of an apparent attempt to "break away" from the National Wrestling Alliance by, not only Southwest Wrestling (Joe Blanchard), but an alliance with Georgia Championship Wrestling, Angelo Poffo's International Championship Wrestling (ICW), Don Owen's Pacific Northwest Wrestling, Bill Watts' Mid-South wrestling, and possibly Jerry Jarrett in Memphis. The groups begin working closely with one another, even co-promoting some shows in Texas, and, Dave Meltzer even writes, that Georgia wrestling didn't immediately announce Harley Race winning the NWA World title from Ric Flair. Ultimately, nothing came out of the situation. Southwest wrestling was in financial trouble and dropped their "undisputed" world championship by the fall. This story is chronicled in our review of the 1983 *Wrestling Observer Newsletter* on our Patreon membership page at WhenItWasCool.com.

05-22-1983: AWA in St. Paul, MN: Brad Rheingans beat John Tolos... Kenny Jay beat Sgt. Rene Goulet... Baron Von Raschke beat Jesse Ventura... Buck Zumhofe beat Mike Graham by DQ... Jim Brunzell beat Ken Patera by DQ... Wahoo McDaniel & Rick Martel beat Nick Bockwinkel & Blackjack Lanza... Mad Dog Vachon beat Jerry Blackwell.

05-23-1983: WWF at Madison Square Garden in New York City, NY: WWF champion Bob Backlund defeated Sgt. Slaughter by DQ... WWF Intercontinental champion Don Muraco battled Rocky Johnson to a draw... Dusty Rhodes defeated The Samoan III (Samu Anoa'i)... Jimmy Snuka defeated Wild Samoan Afa... Ivan Koloff defeated Jules Strongbow... Jay Strongbow battled Iron Mike Sharpe to a no contest... Fabulous Moolah defeated Princess Victoria... Don Kernodle defeated Baron Mikel Scicluna... Salvatore Bellomo defeated Swede Hanson... Susan Starr defeated Leilani Kai... Jose Luis Rivera defeated Pete Doherty.

One Man Gang & Kelly Kiniski win the Mid-Atlantic tag team titles in a tournament in Greenville, SC for Jim Crockett Promotions by defeating Jimmy Valiant & Bugsy McGraw and Mike Rotundo & Rufus R. Jones.

Rick Gibson defeats The Flame (Jody Hamilton) for the Alabama title in Birmingham, AL. On the same show NWA World heavyweight champion Ric Flair defeated Austin Idol to retain the title.

In Memphis, TN: Mid-South Coliseum drawing 5,816: Sonny King beat King Cobra... The Lone Ranger (Stan Frazier) beat Mad Dog... The Galaxians (Ken Wayne & Danny Davis) beat Carl Fergie & Bobby Fulton... Porkchop Cash & Dream Machine (Troy Graham) beat Terry Taylor & Steve O... Mid-America champion Stagger Lee (Koko Ware) beat The Ace of Spades (Tommy Gilbert) in a mask vs. mask match… The Grapplers (Len Denton & Tony Anthony) beat The Rock-n-Roll Express (Ricky Morton & Robert Gibson) in a no DQ match… The Fabulous Ones (Steve Keirn & Stan Lane) beat Southern tag team champions Duke Myers & Bobby Eaton via DQ… Dutch Mantel beat Bill Dundee in a bull whip match to win the Southern title… CWA International champion Ken Patera beat Jerry Lawler.

JCP: Greenville, SC: Memorial Auditorium: Great Kabuki defeated NWA TV champion Jos LeDuc to win the title.

05-27-1983: Wahoo McDaniel defeated AWA World heavyweight champion Nick Bockwinkel by DQ in Denver, CO.

05-29-1983: NWA U.S. Champion Greg Valentine defeated NWA World heavyweight champion Ric Flair in Asheville, NC for Jim Crockett Promotions but only the U.S. title was at stake.

Leo Burke defeated Johnny Weaver for the North American title in Toronto, Canada at the Maple Leaf Gardens. On the same show NWA World heavyweight champion Ric Flair defeated NWA U.S. champion Greg Valentine.

05-30-1983: In Memphis, TN at Mid-South Coliseum: The Fabulous Ones (Steve Keirn & Stan Lane) beat Bobby Eaton & Duke Myers in a hair vs. title match to win the Southern tag team titles… Bill Dundee beat Jerry Lawler to win the Southern title.

05-31-1983: Georgia Championship Wrestling co-holder of the NWA National tag team titles, Matt Borne, is accused of sexually assaulting a 16 year old girl in Ohio. He was fired by booker Ole Anderson and stripped of the tag team titles with Arn Anderson. Charges against Borne are dropped the following month after the accuser fails to appear at the trial.

05-1983: Mr. Olympia wrestles throughout the summer in the Florida territory but is actually Tommy Wright instead of Jerry Stubbs.

June 1983

06-01-1983: Following a Georgia Championship Wrestling show in Reynoldsburg, OH (suburb of Columbus), Matt Borne is accused of molesting a 16 year old girl. Charges were ultimately dropped but this led to him being fired from Georgia Championship Wrestling and the ending of his team with Arn Anderson. This led directly to the creation of The Road Warriors (Hawk & Animal) as replacements, who went on to become one of the most popular tag teams of all time.

06-02-1983: Jerry Lawler defeated Bill Dundee for the Southern title in Lexington, KY.

New Japan Pro Wrestling: in Tokyo, Japan: Sumo Hall drawing 13,000: Shown June 3, 1983 on TV: Nobuhiko Takada pinned Kazuo Yamazaki... Ryuma Go pinned Yoshiaki Fujiwara... Osamu Kido & Kantaro Hoshino beat El Canek & Enrique Vera... Akira Maeda & Kengo Kimura beat Rusher Kimura & Isamu Teranishi... Seiji Sakaguchi battled Big John Studd to a double count out... Andre the Giant pinned Killer Khan... Tiger Mask (Satoru Sayama) pinned Kuniaki Kobayashi to win the vacant NWA World Junior Heavyweight title... **Hulk Hogan** beat Antonio Inoki via countout to become the first IWGP champion. The match was worked to appear as though it had turned into a shoot knockout of Inoki.

DragonKingKarl Note: It's no wonder Hulk Hogan became the biggest pop culture crossover star that pro wrestling had ever seen up to this point. Following his rise through 1982 and 1983 is interesting. Hulk Hogan is often headlining AWA shows and is even teasing multiple times that he is winning or has won the AWA World heavyweight title. His 1982 appearance as Thunderlips in the movie *Rocky III* exposed him to mainstream popular culture. Now, here in the early summer of 1983, he became New Japan's "Champion of Champions" so-to-speak by winning the inaugural IWGP title tournament by defeating Antonio Inoki in the finals. The finish of the match became part of pro wrestling lore. Hulk Hogan hits Antonio Inoki, who is standing on the ring apron and knocks him to the concrete floor. Inoki starts convulsing and biting his tongue. For many years this was told in pro wrestling circles as an unintended accident. However, many years later, it was finally admitted to being worked. A finish to a match that not only put Hulk Hogan over huge with a controversial win but also saved Antonio Inoki from doing a clean loss.

06-04-1983: The Southern title loss from Bill Dundee to Jerry Lawler is repeated in Nashville, TN this time with a loser leaves town stipulation added.

06-05-1983: A tournament for the NWA National heavyweight title is held in Atlanta, GA at the Omni. Results: Larry Zbyszko defeated Brett Wayne (Brett

Wayne Sawyer, the brother of Buzz Sawyer)... Tommy Rich defeated The Super Destroyer (Scott Irwin)... Masked Superstar (Bill Eadie) defeated Ray Candy... Paul Ellering battled Ole Anderson to a double DQ... Stan Hansen defeated Pat Rose... Ronnie Garvin defeated Mike Starbuck... Mr. Wrestling II (Johnny Walker) defeated Bob Roop... Arn Anderson defeated Mark Hill... Pez Whatley defeated Tracey Stone... Round 2: Larry Zbyszko defeated Tommy Rich by count out... Iron Sheik defeated Ronnie Garvin... Mr. Wrestling II (Johnny Walker) defeated Arn Anderson... Buzz Sawyer defeated Pez Whatley... Dick Murdoch defeated Killer Tim Brooks... Round 3: Larry Zbyszko defeated Masked Superstar (Bill Eadie) by count out... Stan Hansen defeated the Iron Sheik... Buzz Sawyer battled Dick Murdoch to a double DQ... Semi-Finals: Larry Zbyszko defeated Stan Hansen by count out... Finals: Larry Zbyszko defeated Mr. Wrestling II (Johnny Walker) to win the National heavyweight title... In a boxing tag team match Dick Murdoch & Ernie Shavers defeated Buzz Sawyer & Killer Tim Brooks by count out.

06-06-1983: In Memphis, TN: Mid-South Coliseum drawing 11,300: Galaxian 2 (Ken Wayne) beat Steve O... Tommy Gilbert beat Galaxian 1 (Danny Davis)... Tom Prichard beat Carl Fergie... Dutch Mantel & Penny Mitchell beat Joyce Grable & The Angel... The Rock-n-Roll Express (Ricky Morton & Robert Gibson) & Terry Taylor & Stagger Lee (Koko Ware) beat Porkchop Cash & Dream Machine (Troy Graham) & The Grapplers (Len Denton & Tony Anthony)... The Fabulous Ones (Steve Keirn & Stan Lane) beat Bobby Eaton & Duke Myers & Jim Cornette & Jimmy Hart in a handicap match... Jerry Lawler beat Bill Dundee to win the Southern title in a no DQ loser leaves town match.

06-07-1983: The Southern title loss from Bill Dundee to Jerry Lawler is repeated in Louisville, KY this time with a loser leaves town stipulation added.

06-08-1983: All-Japan Pro Wrestling: in Tokyo, Japan: Sumo Hall drawing 12,500: Mitsuo Momota pinned Toshiaki Kawada... Ultra 7 pinned Nobuyoshi Suguwara... Shiro Koshinaka pinned Masaji Gotoh... Nikolai Volkoff & The Destroyer (Dick Beyer) beat Motoshi Okuma & The Great Kojika... Takashi Ishikawa & Ashura Hara beat Roddy Piper & Bill Irwin... NWA International Junior champion Chavo Guerrero battled Mighty Inoue to a double count out... Genichiro Tenryu pinned Dick Slater... PWF champion Giant Baba battled Bruiser Brody to a double DQ... NWA World champion Ric Flair drew Jumbo Tsuruta.

06-10-1983: Missouri & Central States champion **Harley Race** defeats NWA World heavyweight champion Ric Flair to win the world title in St. Louis, MO.

DragonKingKarl Note: This was a huge, historic win for Harley Race as this made him the first ever seven-time NWA World heavyweight champion beating the former record held by Lou Thesz (though the Lou Thesz "6 time" designation was actually a combination of multiple world championships. Lou Thesz only technically held the 1948 version of the National Wrestling Alliance World title three times. It should be noted, however, that Lou Thesz held the world title far longer in the number of days held than Harley Race ever did). This also ended Ric Flair's first run as NWA World champion and set up a five month title chase that would end in November at the first Starrcade supershow. During this chase, Ric Flair would win the NWA Missouri title, face Harley Race in front of large attendances in Toronto and the Mid-Atlantic area, and have Harley Race put a bounty on Ric Flair in storyline. Harley Race would eventually win the NWA World heavyweight title again in an unreported (at the time) quick title change in New Zealand in 1984 with Ric Flair recapturing it in Singapore three days later.

06-11-1983: Duke Myers & Bobby Eaton lose the Southern tag team titles to the Fabulous Ones (Steve Keirn & Stan Lane) in Nashville, TN.

WWF: Boston, MA: Boston Garden: Attendance 13,198: Salvatore Bellomo wrestled Samula to a draw… Butcher Vachon defeats Fred Marzino… Iron Mike Sharpe defeats Pete Doherty… Don Kernodle defeats Mac Rivera… Chief Jay Strongbow & Jimmy Snuka defeat WWF Tag Team champions The Wild Samoans (Afa & Sika) by DQ… Sgt. Slaughter defeats WWF champion Bob Backlund by Count Out… Swede Hanson defeats Baron Mikel Scicluna… Andre the Giant defeats Big John Studd.

The Road Warriors (Hawk & Animal) makes their tag team debut on WTBS at the WTBS Studios in Atlanta, GA defeating Joe Young & Randy Barber. They debut as the NWA National tag team champions after being awarded the titles following the firing of Matt Borne.

DragonKingKarl Note: I was a huge fan of The Road Warriors. I first became aware of them via the newsstand magazines. They looked incredible and the magazines put them over big time. By the time I finally got to see them wrestle on television several months later (at a friend's house who had TBS) I was blown away. I couldn't care less that they "couldn't work a lick" according to experts. I was a kid. The story was that they were an unstoppable wrecking machine of a tag team and they were. And... they looked the part. They had charisma in spades and looked unstoppable. I remained a Road Warriors fan for the rest of the time they were in wrestling. Sadly, both Hawk (Michael Hegstrand) and Animal (Joe Laurinitis) have passed away, but I remain a steadfast fan of The Road Warriors / Legion of Doom.

06-12-1983: UWA Mexico: in Mexico City, Mexico: El Toreo drawing 30,000: Dr. Wagner Jr. & Scorpio & Tamba beat Black Man & Enrique Vera & Junji Hirata... Babe Face & Perro Aguayo beat George Takano & Gran Hamada... Hiro Saito & Kotetsu Yamamoto & Norio Honaga beat Anibal & El Solitario & Villano III... Tiger Mask beat Fishman to win the vacant WWF Junior Heavyweight title... El Canek beat Tatsumi Fujinami to win the UWA Heavyweight title.

06-13-1983: In Memphis, TN: Mid-South Coliseum drawing 5,716: Don Anderson beat Bruise Brother 2... Tommy Gilbert beat Galaxian 1 (Danny Davis)... Tom Prichard pinned Jimmy Kent... The Grapplers (Len Denton & Tony Anthony) beat The Rock-n-Roll Express (Ricky Morton & Robert Gibson) in a match where the Grapplers' masks were at stake... Mid-America champion Stagger Lee (Koko Ware) beat Bruise Brother 1 in a mask vs. $500 match... Dutch Mantel & Penny Mitchell beat Duke Myers & Joyce Grable... Bobby Eaton pinned Mad Dog in a mad dog match... The Moondogs (Rex & Spot) battled The Fabulous Ones (Steve Keirn & Stan Lane) to a double DQ... Man Mountain Link pinned Jerry Lawler to win the Southern title... Stagger Lee (Koko Ware) won a battle royal.

Rick Martel defeated AWA World champion Nick Bockwinkel by DQ in Salt Lake City, UT.

Southwest Wrestling (Joe Blanchard Promotion) in San Antonio, TX: Tully Blanchard defeated Bob Sweetan to win the Southwest heavyweight title.

06-17-1983: 21,000 fans turn out to Reunion Arena in Dallas, TX for World Class Championship Wrestling (WCCW) Star Wars. Results: Genichiro Tenryu defeated Johnny Mantell… Vickie Carranza defeated Lola Gonzales… Jose Lothario & Chris Adams & Chavo Guerrero defeated Bill Irwin & Fishman & The Mongol… Buddy Roberts defeated Iceman King Parsons in a hair vs hair match. Despite winning the match, Roberts had hair remover rubbed all over his head… David Von Erich defeated Jimmy Garvin via DQ per match stipulations Sunshine became David's valet for a day… All Japan United National Champion Jumbo Tsuruta defeated Ted DiBiase… PWF champion Giant Baba defeated King Kong Bundy… Kamala defeated Armand Hussein & Tola Yatsu (Yoshiaki Yatsu) & Mike Bond in a handicap match… NWA World heavyweight champion Harley Race defeated Kevin Von Erich via DQ… Kerry Von Erich & Bruiser Brody defeated Michael Hayes & Terry Gordy to win the American tag team titles.

WWF in New York City, NY at Madison Square Garden. Results: Iron Mike Sharpe defeated SD Jones… Swede Hanson defeated Butcher Vachon… Salvatore Bellomo defeated Mr. Fuji by DQ… Ivan Koloff defeated Tony Garea… George Steele defeated Chief Jay Strongbow… Ivan Putski & Jimmy Snuka & Rocky Johnson defeated Don Muraco & Wild Samoans in a best 2 out of 3 falls match…

Andre the Giant defeated Big John Studd… Sgt. Slaughter defeated WWF champion Bob Backlund by countout.

AWA in Denver, CO: Brad Rheingans beat Chris Markoff… Greg Gagne beat Mike Graham… Ken Patera beat Jim Brunzell… Baron Von Raschke & Wahoo McDaniel beat Nick Bockwinkel & Blackjack Lanza… Mad Dog Vachon beat Jerry Blackwell.

Sexual assault charges against Matt Borne are dropped in Franklin County Ohio Municipal Court when the defendant and her mother fail to appear. The mother had been dating Borne at the time the alleged assault took place on June 1.

06-18-1983: Jack & Jerry Brisco defeated Ricky Steamboat & Jay Youngblood to win the NWA World tag team titles in Greenville, SC.

AWA in Chicago, IL: Brad Rheingans beat Chris Markoff… Mike Graham beat Nacho Barrera… Rick Martel beat Bob Colt… Ken Patera beat Jim Brunzell… Greg Gagne beat Bobby Heenan… Wahoo McDaniel & Jerry Lawler & Dick the Bruiser beat Nick Bockwinkel & Jesse Ventura & Blackjack Lanza… Mad Dog Vachon beat Jerry Blackwell.

06-19-1983: GCW at the Omni in Atlanta, GA: Mr. Wrestling II (Johnny Walker) defeated Larry Zbyszko by DQ… Mr. Wrestling II defeated Killer Tim Brooks… Loser Leaves Town: Strap Match: Buzz Sawyer defeated Dick Murdoch… Ronnie Garvin defeated Iron Sheik… Stan Hansen & Tommy Rich defeated National tag team champions The Road Warriors (Hawk & Animal) by DQ… Pez Whatley defeated Super Destroyer (Scott Irwin)... Bill Irwin defeated Joe Lightfoot... Rick Rude defeated Bob Roop.

In Orlando, FL: NWA World heavyweight champion Harley Race defeated Dusty Rhodes with Ron Bass as special referee.

In Hamburg, MN: Buck Zumhofe defeated Mike Graham for the AWA World Junior title.

06-20-1983: In Memphis, TN: Mid-South Coliseum drawing 6,525: Don Anderson & Ken Timbs beat The A-Team (Don Bass & Roger Smith)... Tom Prichard beat The Giant Rebel (Stan Frazier)... Stagger Lee (Koko Ware) & Dutch Mantel beat Porkchop Cash & Dream Machine (Troy Graham)... Mad Dog pinned Bobby Eaton in a mad dog match... The Rock-n-Roll Express (Ricky Morton & Robert Gibson) beat The Grapplers (Len Denton & Tony Anthony) in a Texas death match... The Fabulous Ones (Steve Keirn & Stan Lane) battled The Moondogs (Rex & Spot) to a double DQ in a lumberjack match... Jerry Lawler beat Man Mountain Link to win the Southern title... Jerry Lawler beat CWA International champion Ken Patera via DQ.

In West Palm Beach, FL: NWA World heavyweight champion Harley Race defeated Barry Windham.

In San Antonio, TX: Dick Murdoch defeated Adrian Adonis to win Southwest World heavyweight title but the belt was later held up.

06-21-1983: In Tampa, FL at the Fort Hesterly Armory: NWA World heavyweight champion Harley Race defeated Scott McGhee.

06-22-1983: In Miami Beach, FL at the Convention Center: NWA World heavyweight champion Harley Race defeated Dusty Rhodes.

06-24-1983: AWA in St. Paul, MN: Chris Markoff beat Tom Stone… Brad Rheingans beat Rick Martel… Mr. Saito beat Buck Zumhofe… Bobby Heenan beat Kenny Jay… Baron Von Raschke beat Blackjack Lanza by DQ… Ken Patera & Jerry Blackwell beat Greg Gagne & Jim Brunzell to win the AWA World tag team titles… AWA World heavyweight champion Nick Bockwinkel beat Wahoo McDaniel.

WWF: Pittsburgh, PA: Civic Arena: Attendance: 18,000: Johnny DeFazio pinned the Beast… Mr. Fuji fought Chief Jay Strongbow to a draw… Mike Skully defeated Bill Dixon… WWF Intercontinental champion Don Muraco defeated Rocky Johnson in a steel cage match… Andre the Giant defeated Big John Studd via count-out… Salvatore Bellomo pinned Baron Mikel Scicluna… Iron Mike Sharpe pinned SD Jones… Jimmy Snuka & Ivan Putski defeated WWF tag team champions the Wild Samoans (Afa & Sika) by DQ.

Arn Anderson returns briefly to Mid-South wrestling where he had previously wrestled as Marty Lunde and debuts his new Arn Anderson name and storyline relation to the Anderson family on a Mid-South television show from the Irish McNeil's Boys Club in Shreveport, LA when he takes on NWA National champion Mr. Wrestling II (Johnny Walker) on the show.

DragonKingKarl Note: Poor Arn Anderson's career took a major detour in 1983 thanks to Matt Borne. Marty Lunde had been going nowhere in Bill Watts' Mid-South promotion until one day, in the dressing room, the Junkyard Dog pointed out to Bill Watts that Lunde looked a lot like Arn Anderson. The ever creative Bill Watts' brain kicked into gear and sent Lunde to Georgia where he became the cousin or nephew or whatever (it varied) of Ole Anderson. Rebranded as Arn (Arnold) Anderson, he was teamed up with another up-and-comer, second generation wrestler Matt Borne, son of "Tough" Tony Borne. The two became NWA National tag team champions until Matt Borne was accused of sexual assault in Ohio and fired. Arn Anderson remained in Georgia for several weeks but went nowhere. He ends up back in Mid-South for a short time, now known as Arn Anderson, but soon departs for Ron Fuller's Southeastern Championship Wrestling (SECW) promotion under a mask as Super Olympia, a dopple-ganger for Mr. Olympia (Jerry Stubbs). Both Super Olympia and Mr. Olympia were babyfaces and it seemed in storyline that Mr. Olympia was unaware of the existence of fellow good-guy Super Olympia. You knew a turn from someone was coming. Few expected it to be from Mr. Olympia. A newly heel Mr. Olympia entered a feud with Super Olympia and eventually lost his mask to the newcomer. The Jerry Stubbs verses Super Olympia feud continued for a while before they transitioned to different opponents for a while. Super Olympia found himself at odds with another fellow babyface, Jacques Rougeau. Jacques Rougeau then took the mask from Super Olympia revealing him to be Arn Anderson. Arn Anderson eventually began teaming with his former rival Jerry Stubbs and the two became one of the best tag teams the area had seen. Arn Anderson talks glowingly about his time in Southeastern, calling it one of the best times of his life. While professionally, it may have seemed like a time-out, personally it worked out well and led to him meeting his long time friend Ric Flair who eventually brought him to Jim Crockett Promotions which then led to the creation of the Four Horsemen.

06-25-1983: In Orlando, FL: NWA World heavyweight champion Harley Race defeated Barry Windham by DQ.

JCP: Charlotte, NC: Coliseum: Attendance: 6,819: Rick McCord defeated Masa Fuchi… Mike Rotundo defeated Kelly Kiniski… Jos LeDuc defeated One Man Gang… Jake Roberts defeated Bob Orton Jr… Rufus R. Jones defeated Magic Dragon… NWA TV champion Great Kabuki defeated Jimmy Valiant… Ric Flair & Roddy Piper defeated Greg Valentine & Dory Funk Jr… NWA World tag team champions Jack & Jerry Brisco defeated Ricky Steamboat & Jay Youngblood.

06-26-1983: WWF champion Bob Backlund defeated WWF Intercontinental champion Don Muraco in Salisbury, MD.

Ken Patera & Jerry Blackwell defeated Greg Gagne & Jim Brunzell to win the AWA World tag team titles in St. Paul, MN. On the same show with an attendance of 14,000: AWA World champion Nick Bockwinkel defeated Wahoo McDaniel… Baron Von Raschke battled Blackjack Lanza to a no contest… Bobby Heenan defeated Kenny Jay… Buck Zumhofe defeated Mr. Saito via DQ… Brad Rheingans battled Rick Martel to a draw.

06-27-1983: In Memphis, TN: Mid-South Coliseum drawing 6,917: Ted Allen pinned The Galaxian (Danny Davis)… Don Anderson beat Ken Timbs… The Grapplers (Len Denton & Tony Anthony) pinned Tommy Gilbert & Dutch

Mantel... Tom Prichard pinned Duke Myers... Little Tokyo beat Chilly Bo Diddley... Porkchop Cash & Dream Machine (Troy Graham) beat The Rock-n-Roll Express (Ricky Morton & Robert Gibson)... Bobby Eaton & Jimmy Hart beat Mad Dog & Stagger Lee (Koko Ware)... Jerry Lawler & Austin Idol beat Ken Patera & Man Mountain Link... The Fabulous Ones (Steve Keirn & Stan Lane) beat The Moondogs (Rex & Spot) via DQ in a steel cage match.

July 1983

07-02-1983: In Atlanta, GA on WTBS TV Mr. Wrestling II (Johnny Walker) defeated Larry Zbyszko in a mask vs $25,000 challenge elimination match.

WWF: Los Angeles, CA: Sports Arena: Attendance: 9,100: Alexis Smirnoff defeated Jerry Monti... Black Gordman & Goliath defeated Steve Pardee & Billy Anderson... Mil Mascaras defeated Ivan Koloff via DQ... Tony Atlas defeated Jack Armstrong... Pat Patterson defeated Buddy Rose... Jimmy Snuka defeated Mr. Fuji... Andre the Giant defeated Big John Studd via count-out in a $10,000 bodyslam match... WWF champion Bob Backlund fought Sgt. Slaughter via DQ.

07-03-1983: At the Omni in Atlanta, GA Mr. Wrestling II (Johnny Walker) defeated Larry Zbyszko to win the NWA National heavyweight title. Attendance was 4,000.

07-04-1983: World Class Championship Wrestling: Independence Day Star Wars: in Fort Worth, TX: Convention Center drawing 12,000: Michael Hayes pinned Iceman Parsons in a lights out match... Bruiser Brody battled Kamala to a double DQ... David Von Erich beat Jimmy Garvin to win the held-up World Class Texas title... The Von Erichs (Kevin & David & Kerry Von Erich) defeat World Class World 6-Man tag team titles The Fabulous Freebirds (Terry Gordy & Michael Hayes & Buddy Roberts) to win the titles 2 falls to 1.

In Memphis, TN: Mid-South Coliseum drawing 8,774: Ken Timbs beat Ted Allen... Tommy Gilbert beat The Galaxian (Danny Davis)... Duke Myers wrestled Dutch Mantel to a draw... Tom Prichard & Chief Lone Eagle beat The Giant Rebel (Stan Frazier) & Little Tokyo... The Rock-n-Roll Express (Ricky Morton & Robert Gibson) & Steve Regal & Spike Huber & Mad Dog beat Man Mountain Link & Dream Machine (Troy Graham) & Porkchop Cash & The Grapplers (Len Denton & Tony Anthony)... Frankie Laine beat Stagger Lee (Koko Ware) to win the Mid-America title... The Fabulous Ones (Steve Keirn & Stan Lane) & Austin Idol beat The Moondogs (Rex & Spot) & Bobby Eaton in a steel cage match... Jimmy Hart & Andy Kaufman beat Jerry Lawler via DQ... Jerry Lawler won a battle royal for a new Corvette.

07-05-1983: Scott McGhee & Mike Graham defeated Angelo Mosca & Bobby Duncum to win the Global tag team titles in Tampa, FL.

07-06-1983: In Miami Beach, FL at the Convention Center: Attendance: 5,676: Dusty Rhodes defeated Ox Baker by DQ... Purple Haze (Mark Lewin) battled Blackjack Mulligan to a no contest... Barry Windham defeated Ron Bass... Mike Graham & Brad Armstrong & Scott McGhee defeated Adrian Street & Bobby Duncum & Elijah Akeem (Ray Candy)... Charlie Cook battled Les Thornton to a draw... Penny Mitchell defeated Joyce Grable... Kevin Sullivan defeated Denny Brown... Adrian Street defeated Bob Russell.

07-09-1983: WWF: Boston, MA: Boston Garden: Attendance: 14,820: Swede Hanson defeated Frank Williams... Tito Santana defeated Pete Doherty... Salvatore Bellomo fought Iron Mike Sharpe to a draw... WWF Intercontinental champion Don Muraco fought Jimmy Snuka to a no contest... WWF World tag team champions the Wild Samoans (Afa & Sika) defeated Tony Garea & Mac Rivera... WWF champion Bob Backlund defeated George Steele via count-out... Rocky Johnson fought Big John Studd to a double DQ... Ivan Putski defeated Ivan Koloff via count-out... **The Invaders (Jose Gonzalez & Johnny Rivera)** defeated Bob Bradley & Mr. Fuji.

DragonKingKarl Note: The Invaders came to the WWF with a solid push and the possibility of becoming WWF World tag team champions. For whatever reason, this never materialized and the team settled into the mid-cards. In the WWF and in World Wrestling Council (WWC) the Invader 1 was Jose Gonzalez, who infamously would kill Bruiser Brody in a locker room attack in 1988. The Invader 2 in WWF was Johnny Rivera, yet in Puerto Rico, The Invader 2 was Roberto Soto and Johnny Rivera was The Invader 3.

07-10-1983: 20,703 fans turn out to Toronto Exhibition Stadium in Toronto, Canada. Results: Nick DeCarlo & Billy Red Lyons defeated The Executioner (unknown) & Bill Armstrong... Kelly Kiniski & Rene Goulet defeated Bob & Joe Marcus to retain the Mid-Atlantic tag team titles... Johnny Weaver & Mike Rotunda defeated Alec & Tim Gerrard... Fabulous Moolah defeated Princess Victoria to retain the Women's World championship... Dick Slater defeated Nick DeCarlo... Great Kabuki defeated Jimmy Valiant to retain the Mid-Atlantic TV title... Ricky Steamboat & Jay Youngblood defeated Jake Roberts & Dory Funk

Jr... Angelo Mosca defeated One Man Gang to retain the Canadian heavyweight title... NWA U.S. champion Greg Valentine battled Wahoo McDaniel to a double count out... Ric Flair defeated NWA World heavyweight champion Harley Race by DQ.

07-11-1983: AWA in Salt Lake City, UT: Attendance: 7900: David Schultz beat Buck Zumhofe... Greg Gagne beat Mr. Saito by DQ... Jim Brunzell beat Jerry Blackwell... Ken Patera beat Mad Dog Vachon... Rick Martel & Wahoo McDaniel beat Bobby Heenan & Blackjack Lanza.

In Memphis, TN: Mid-South Coliseum drawing 7,466: Spike Huber drew Don Anderson... Sweet Daddy O beat Tommy Gilbert... The Jaguar (Danny Davis) beat Ken Timbs... Tom Prichard pinned Apocalypse (Mike Boyer)... The Rock-n-Roll Express (Ricky Morton & Robert Gibson) beat Duke Myers & Man Mountain Link... Mid-America champion Frankie Laine pinned Dutch Mantel... The Grapplers (Len Denton & Tony Anthony) beat The Fabulous Ones (Steve Keirn & Stan Lane) to win the Southern tag team titles... Porkchop Cash & Dream Machine (Troy Graham) beat Jerry Lawler & Austin Idol... The Moondogs (Rex & Spot) beat Stagger Lee (Koko Ware) & Bobby Eaton via DQ... Andy Kaufman beat Jimmy Hart via DQ in a lights out match.

WWF: East Rutherford, NJ: Meadowlands: Attendance: 21,400; sell out: Jeff Craney pinned Pete Doherty... Tito Santana pinned Don Kernodle... Tony Garea fought Mr. Fuji to a time-limit draw... Salvatore Bellomo defeated Iron Mike Sharpe via DQ... Ivan Putski pinned Samula... WWF tag team champions the Wild Samoans (Afa & Sika) defeated The Invaders (Jose Gonzalez & Johnny

Rivera)... Rocky Johnson pinned Ivan Koloff... Andre the Giant defeated Big John Studd in a steel cage match... WWF champion Bob Backlund pinned Sgt. Slaughter in a Texas Death Match.

07-14-1983: In Winnipeg, Canada, Verne Gagne comes back out of retirement to team with Mad Dog Vachon and defeat AWA World tag team champions Ken Patera & Jerry Blackwell in a non-title match. Also on the show: Wahoo McDaniel & Baron Von Raschke defeated Blackjack Lanza & Bobby Heenan... Greg Gagne defeated Sheik Adnan... Mr. Saito defeated Buck Zumhofe... Rick Martel battled Bill White to a draw... David Schultz defeated Brad Rheingans.

WWF: Glens Falls, NY: Civic Center: Attendance: 7,000: Salvatore Bellomo defeated Chico Rodriguez... The Invaders (Jose Gonzalez & Johnny Rivera) defeated Salvatore Bellomo & Swede Hanson... Rocky Johnson defeated Ivan Koloff... Andre the Giant fought Big John Studd to a double count-out... WWF champion Bob Backlund defeated George Steele.

07-15-1983: George Steele defeated WWF champion Bob Backlund by DQ in Portland, ME.

AWA in Denver, CO: Wahoo McDaniel beat Bobby Jaggers... Rick Martel beat David Schultz... Mr. Saito beat Buck Zumhofe... Brad Rheingans beat Bill White... Wahoo McDaniel beat Bobby Heenan in a lumberjack Match... Greg Gagne & Jim Brunzell beat Tully Blanchard & Bobby Jaggers.

In St. Louis, MO **Ric Flair** wins the NWA Missouri title in a tournament defeating Bob Brown, George Wells, Butch Reed, and David Von Erich. Also on the show Hulk Hogan fought Jerry Blackwell to a no contest.

DragonKingKarl Notes: The NWA Missouri championship was often called the "stepping stone to the NWA World title", as part of that story, former world champion Ric Flair wins the Missouri title with the plans being for Flair to regain the title at the first Starrcade supershow in November.

07-16-1983: Mid-South wrestling at the New Orleans, LA Superdome: 19,000: Butch Reed defeats Junkyard Dog for the North American title… King Kong Bundy defeated Dusty Rhodes in a taped fist match… Jim Duggan defeated Ted DiBiase in a Lights Out Match… Iceman King Parsons defeated Buddy Roberts… Mr. Wrestling II (Johnny Walker) defeated Larry Zbyszko… Tommy Rich defeated Kamala… Magnum T.A. defeated Buzz Sawyer by DQ… Mil Mascaras & Tim Horner defeated Mr. Olympia (Jerry Stubbs) & Boris Zhukov (Jim Nelson)… George Weingroff defeated Art Crews… Johnny Rich defeated Rip Rogers.

WWF: Philadelphia, PA: Spectrum: Attendance: 10,000: Televised on the PRISM Network: Swede Hanson defeated Jeff Craney… Iron Mike Sharpe pinned Tony Garea… Tito Santana defeated Don Kernodle… WWF Intercontinental champion Don Muraco defeated Jimmy Snuka via DQ… Sgt. Slaughter defeated SD Jones… WWF champion Bob Backlund pinned George Steele… The Invaders (Jose Gonzalez & Johnny Rivera) defeated Mr. Fuji & Frank Williams… Ivan Koloff defeated Salvatore Bellomo… Airing on All American Wrestling - 10/9/83: Andre the Giant & Ivan Putski & Chief Jay Strongbow & Rocky Johnson defeated Big John Studd & Samula & The Wild Samoans (Afa & Sika).

07-17-1983: GCW at the Omni in Atlanta, GA Ronnie Garvin defeated the Iron Sheik to win the NWA National TV title in a no time limit match... In a Lights Out Match: Mr. Wrestling II (Johnny Walker) defeated Larry Zbyszko by DQ... Mr. Wrestling II defeated Killer Tim Brooks... Texas Death Match: Buzz Sawyer defeated Tommy Rich... Pez Whatley defeated Larry Zbyszko... The Road Warriors (Hawk & Animal) defeated Steve O & Terry Taylor... Arn Anderson & Rick Rude defeated Carl Fergie & Norman Fredrick Charles III... Bill Irwin defeated Joe Lightfoot... Brett Wayne defeated Pat Rose.

In Orlando, FL: WWF champion Bob Backlund defeated Ron Bass by DQ.

07-18-1983: In Memphis, TN: Mid-South Coliseum drawing 6,790: Tom Prichard drew Duke Myers... The Jaguar (Danny Davis) beat The Galaxian (Ken Wayne)... The Giant Rebel (Stan Frazier) won an elimination match: Also in the match were: Don Anderson, Tommy Gilbert, Spike Huber, Man Mountain Link, Mad Dog, Duke Myers, Sweet Daddy O, Tom Prichard, and Ken Timbs... Dutch Mantel beat Frankie Laine to win the Mid-America title... CWA tag team champions The Assassins (Don Bass & Roger Smith) beat The Rock-n-Roll Express (Ricky Morton & Robert Gibson)... The Moondogs (Rex & Spot) beat Bobby Eaton & Stagger Lee (Koko Ware) in a no DQ match... Southern tag team champions The Grapplers (Len Denton & Tony Anthony) beat The Fabulous Ones (Steve Keirn & Stan Lane) via DQ... Jerry Lawler & Austin Idol beat Porkchop Cash & Dream

Machine (Troy Graham)... Jerry Lawler & Andy Kaufman beat Assassin 1 (Don Bass) & Jimmy Hart via DQ.

In West Palm Beach, FL: WWF champion Bob Backlund defeated Bobby Duncum.

07-19-1983: Jos LeDuc defeated Scott McGhee on TV in Tampa, FL for the Florida title. Also, WWF champion Bob Backlund defeated Ron Bass by DQ.

07-20-1983: In Miami Beach, FL at the Convention Center: Attendance: 5,543: Blackjack Mulligan & Angelo Mosca defeated Kevin Sullivan & Purple Haze (Mark Lewin)... WWF champion Bob Backlund defeated Ron Bass... Barry Windham & Fabulous Moolah defeated Adrian Street & Miss Linda... Elijah Akeem (Ray Candy) defeated Mike Graham... Scott McGhee defeated Bobby Duncum... Les Thornton & Angelo Mosca, Jr. defeated Ox Baker & Shotgun Willie.

07-22-1983: In Richmond, VA at the Coliseum, Jimmy Valiant defeated One Man Gang & Sir Oliver Humperdink in a handicap hair vs hair loser leaves town steel cage match. Also on the show NWA World heavyweight champion Harley Race defeated Ric Flair by DQ.

WWF: Pittsburgh, PA: Civic Arena: Attendance: 14,000: Don Kernodle pinned Johnny DeFazio... Tito Santana pinned Mr. Fuji... Bill Dixon pinned Bill Berger... Andre the Giant defeated Big John Studd in a Bodyslam match... Chief Jay Strongbow defeated Baron Mikel Scicluna... WWF Intercontinental champion Don Muraco fought Jimmy Snuka to a double DQ... Sgt. Slaughter pinned Tony Garea... WWF champion Bob Backlund pinned George Steele.

07-23-1983: WWF: Landover, MD: Capital Centre: Attendance: 19,800; sell out: Televised on the USA Network... Bob Bradley defeated Steve King... Jeff Craney defeated Jack Carson... Pete Sanchez defeated Israel Matia... Swede Hanson defeated Tony Colon... George Steele defeated Salvatore Bellomo... Rocky Johnson pinned Mr. Fuji... WWF Intercontinental champion Don Muraco fought Jimmy Snuka to a double DQ... Andre the Giant defeated Big John Studd in a steel cage match by escaping through the door after a bodyslam. This match was not televised on USA Network, instead the Samoans vs. Andre the Giant & Dusty Rhodes & Ivan Putski match from Madison Square Garden (July 30, 1983) aired in its place; the cage match later aired alongside the MSG show which took place a week later.

JCP: Charlotte, NC: Coliseum: Attendance: 5,314: Rene Goulet defeated John Bonello... Vinnie Valentino defeated Golden Boy Jerry Grey... Dick Slater & Jake Roberts defeated Johnny Weaver & Brett Hart (Barry Horowitz)... Mid-Atlantic Heavyweight champion Dory Funk Jr. defeated Rufus R Jones... NWA US champion Greg Valentine pinned Roddy Piper... Jimmy Valiant & Bob Orton Jr. defeated Great Kabuki & Gary Hart in a steel cage match... Ric Flair defeated NWA World champion Harley Race via disqualification.

07-24-1983: Return of the Champions: in Toronto, ON: Exhibition Stadium drawing 11,000: NWA US champion Greg Valentine beat Cy Jernigan... One Man Gang beat Mike Davis... Jacques Goulet & Kelly Kiniski beat Nick DeCarlo & Vinnie Valentino... Bob Marcus beat Masa Fuchi... Rufus R. Jones beat Jake Roberts... Mid-Atlantic champion Dory Funk, Jr. pinned Mike Rotunda... NWA World tag team champions Jack & Jerry Brisco beat Ricky Steamboat & Jay

Youngblood via DQ... Jimmy Valiant & Bob Orton, Jr. beat The Great Kabuki & Gary Hart in a steel cage match... Sgt. Slaughter beat Angelo Mosca to win the NWA Canadian title... NWA World champion Harley Race beat Ric Flair via DQ. Johnny Weaver was the guest referee.

In Tulsa, OK Magnum T.A. & Jim Duggan defeated Ted DiBiase & Boris Zhukov (substituting for Mr. Olympia) to win the Mid-South tag team titles.

AWA in St. Paul, MN: Brad Rheingans battled Bill White to a draw... Baron Von Raschke beat Blackjack Lanza... Jim Brunzell beat David Schultz... Mr. Saito beat Rick Martel... Ken Patera & Jerry Blackwell beat Mad Dog Vachon & Dick the Bruiser by DQ... AWA World heavyweight champion Nick Bockwinkel battled Wahoo McDaniel to a double count out.

07-25-1983: At the Mid-South Coliseum in Memphis, TN: Jerry Lawler defeated Ken Patera for the International title. Also on the show Stagger Lee (Koko Ware) defeated Man Mountain Link in a loser leaves town match. The Fabulous Ones (Steve Keirn & Stan Lane) beat The Grapplers (Len Denton & Tony Anthony) to win the Southern tag team titles.

Montreal, Quebec: Attendance: 18,347: Boo Boucher defeated Tony Rico... Louis Lawrence defeated Mr. Hito via DQ... Tony Parisi & Gino Brito & Armand Rougeau defeated Gilles Poisson & Sailor White & Kurt Von Hess... Rick Martel & Billy Robinson defeated WWF World tag team champions the Wild Samoans (Afa & Sika) via DQ... Abdullah the Butcher defeated Gino Brito... Andre the Giant defeated Blackjack Mulligan via DQ... Dino Bravo defeated the Masked

Superstar (Bill Eadie)... Pat Patterson & Pierre Lefebvre defeated Jacques & Raymond Rougeau.

07-29-1983: Mil Mascaras went to a draw with AWA World heavyweight champion Nick Bockwinkel in Houston, TX. Lou Thesz was the special guest referee.

07-30-1983: WWF in New York City, NY at Madison Square Garden in front of 27,000 fans. Results: Tony Garea went to a time limit draw with Iron Mike Sharpe... Ivan Koloff defeated SD Jones... The Invaders (Jose Gonzalez & Johnny Rivera) defeated Jeff Carney & Gypsy Rodriguez... Big John Studd defeated Salvatore Bellomo... WWF Intercontinental champion Don Muraco battled Jimmy Snuka to a double DQ... Andre the Giant & Dusty Rhodes & Ivan Putski defeated Wild Samoans (Afa & Sika & Samula)... Sgt. Slaughter defeated Swede Hanson... George Steele defeated WWF champion Bob Backlund by DQ... Rocky Johnson defeated Don Kernodle... Tito Santana defeated Mr. Fuji.

07-31-1983: In Orlando, FL: Kareem Muhammad & Elijah Akeem (Leroy Brown & Ray Candy) defeated Scott McGhee & Mike Graham for the Global tag team titles. Also on the show NWA World heavyweight champion Harley Race defeated Dusty Rhodes by DQ.

GCW at the Omni in Atlanta, GA. Attendance: 9,000: Roddy Piper defeated Buzz Sawyer by DQ... The Road Warriors (Hawk & Animal) defeated Jack & Jerry Brisco... Pez Whatley defeated Greg Valentine... Mr. Wrestling II (Johnny Walker) defeated Iron Sheik... Tommy Rich defeated Bill Irwin by DQ... Brett

Wayne battled Ronnie Garvin to a draw... Mr. Wrestling (Tim Woods) defeated Joe Lightfoot... Rick Rude defeated Pat Rose.

August 1983

08-01-1983: In Memphis, TN: Mid-South Coliseum drawing 7,000: The Giant Rebel (Stan Frazier) beat Sweet Daddy O via forfeit... The Rock-n-Roll Express (Ricky Morton & Robert Gibson) & Eddie & Tommy Gilbert beat Ken Timbs & Duke Myers & Porkchop Cash & Dream Machine (Troy Graham)... Buddy Landel beat Steve O... Mid-America champion Dutch Mantel beat Tom Prichard... The Moondogs (Rex & Spot) beat Stagger Lee (Koko Ware) & Bobby Eaton... CWA tag team champions The Assassins (Don Bass & Roger Smith) beat Jerry Lawler & Austin Idol in a no DQ match... The Grapplers (Len Denton & Tony Anthony) beat The Fabulous Ones (Steve Keirn & Stan Lane)... CWA International champion Jerry Lawler beat Ken Patera. Lou Thesz was the special referee.

In West Palm Beach, FL: NWA World heavyweight champion Harley Race battled Mike Graham to a one hour draw.

08-02-1983: In Tampa, FL: NWA World heavyweight champion Harley Race defeated Mike Graham by DQ.

08-03-1983: In Miami Beach, FL at the Convention Center: Attendance: 7,881 (capacity crowd): NWA World heavyweight champion Harley Race defeated Barry Windham by DQ... Dusty Rhodes & Blackjack Mulligan defeated Zambuie Express (Elijah Akeem & Kareem Muhammad / Ray Candy & Leroy Brown) in a steel cage match... Junkyard Dog defeated Ron Bass... Angelo Mosca defeated

Purple Haze (Mark Lewin)... Mil Mascaras defeated Masked Texan... Jos LeDuc defeated Scott McGhee... Mike Graham defeated Ox Baker... Charlie Cook battled Les Thornton to a draw.

08-04-1983: In Jacksonville, FL: NWA World heavyweight champion Harley Race battled Dusty Rhodes to a double DQ.

New Japan Pro Wrestling: in Tokyo, Japan: Sumo Hall drawing 13,000: Shunji Kosugi pinned Nobuhiko Takada... Yoshiaki Fujiwara & Makoto Arakawa beat Haruka Eigen & Yokpalsan... Kuniaki Kobayashi beat Black Cat... Kantaro Hoshino & Osamu Kido beat Pete Roberts & David Finlay... Paul Orndorff pinned Ryuma Go... Kengo Kimura pinned Brian Blair... Seiji Sakaguchi & Akira Maeda beat Dick Murdoch & Adrian Adonis via DQ... Rusher Kimura pinned Animal Hamaguchi in a death match... NWA World Junior Heavyweight champion Tiger Mask (Satoru Sayama) pinned Isamu Teranishi... Tatsumi Fujinami beat Riki Choshu via countout to win the WWF International title.

08-05-1983: In St. Louis, MO NWA World heavyweight champion Harley Race defeated NWA Missouri champion Ric Flair in a best 2 out of 3 falls match.

In Richmond, VA at the Coliseum Rufus R. Jones defeated Dory Funk, Jr. to win the Mid-Atlantic title.

08-07-1983: In Toronto, Canada at the Maple Leaf Gardens a tournament was held for the Canadian TV championship. Mike Rotundo won the tournament defeating Magic Dragon, Sgt. Jacques Goulet, and Don Kernodle.

08-08-1983: At Mid-South Coliseum in Memphis, TN Jerry Lawler & Austin Idol defeated The Assassins (Roger Smith & Don Bass) for the CWA World tag team titles.

In Birmingham, AL for SECW, Ricky Gibson defeated Chick Donovan for the NWA U.S. Junior title. **The Midnight Express** (Norvell Austin & Randy Rose) defeated Ken Lucas & Eddie Hogan (Later Known As: Brutus Beefcake) for the NWA Southeastern tag team titles. Buck Robley defeated The Midnight Stallion (Mongolian Stomper) in a loser leaves town match and in the main event where the loser of the fall must leave town, Ron Fuller & Jimmy Golden defeated Bob Armstrong & The Flame (Jody Hamilton) forcing The Flame to leave town.

DragonKingKarl Notes: 1983 was a very important year for the Midnight Express. At the beginning of 1983 the Midnight Express was a three man Fabulous Freebird style unit consisting of Dennis Condrey & Randy Rose & Norvell Austin in Southeastern Championship Wrestling (SECW) competing in tag team matches where any two of the three could defend the NWA Southeastern tag team titles. One by one members began leaving the territory to go to Jerry Jarrett's Memphis promotion. First, Dennis Condrey, then Norvell Austin (who actually ran over someone with his car and left the area fearing prosecution, or so says Ron Starr in his biography), then later Randy Rose. As each member left they were replaced by new Midnight Express personnel. Eventually the Midnight Express was wrestling in both Memphis and Southeastern with different members. In Memphis it was Dennis Condrey & Norvell Austin and in Southeastern it was Randy Rose & Ron Starr & Wayne Farris (Later Known As: Honky Tonk Man). Then Randy Rose left, leaving Starr & Farris as the Midnight Express then they eventually disbanded. The

Memphis Midnight Express slowly just fell apart. Later in 1983 as part of a talent swap with Bill Watts' Mid-South company, Dennis Condrey and Bobby Eaton, along with manager Jim Cornette went and Watts put them together as a tag team managed by Jim Cornette using the Midnight Express name. This version of the Midnight Express became one of the most popular versions with successful stints in Mid-South, World Class, and eventually Jim Crockett Promotions. Dennis Condrey would then leave Crockett unannounced and would be replaced by Stan Lane who had been part of the Fabulous Ones tag team. Dennis Condrey would reunite with Randy Rose in 1988 as the Original Midnight Express in the AWA and win the AWA World tag team titles. Norvell Austin never again was part of a Midnight Express tag team.

08-12-1983: AWA in Denver, CO: David Schultz beat Buck Zumhofe... Rick Martel beat Mr. Saito by DQ... Jim Brunzell beat Sheik Adnon Al Kaissey... AWA World heavyweight champion Nick Bockwinkel beat Brad Rheingans... Ken Patera & Jerry Blackwell beat Mad Dog Vachon & Baron Von Raschke.

08-13-1983: WWF: Philadelphia, PA: Spectrum: Attendance: 14,008: Televised on the PRISM Network: Pete Sanchez defeated Israel Matea... Tito Santana pinned Mr. Fuji... Big John Studd defeated Chief Jay Strongbow... Jimmy Snuka defeated WWF Intercontinental champion Don Muraco via count-out. Swede Hanson was the guest referee... Tiger Chung Lee defeated Tony Garea via count-out... WWF World tag team champions the Wild Samoans (Afa & Sika) defeated Rocky Johnson & Salvatore Bellomo... Pat Patterson defeated Iron Mike Sharpe... WWF champion Bob Backland defeated Sgt. Slaughter via count-out... The Invaders

(Jose Gonzalez & Johnny Rivera) defeated Ivan Koloff & Don Kernodle... Ivan Putski defeated George Steele.

08-14-1983: GCW at the Omni in Atlanta, GA: Buzz Sawyer defeated Dick Slater by DQ... Pez Whatley defeated Kabuki... NWA World tag team champions Jack & Jerry Brisco defeated The Road Warriors (Hawk & Animal)... Handcuff Match: Tommy Rich defeated Bill Irwin... Mr. Wrestling II (Johnny Walker) battled Larry Zbyszko to a double DQ... Bruno Sammartino, Jr. (David Sammartino) defeated Bob Roop.

In Orlando, FL: NWA World heavyweight champion Harley Race defeated Dusty Rhodes.

08-15-1983: In Memphis, TN: Mid-South Coliseum drawing 6,900: Dream Machine (Troy Graham) & Porkchop Cash & Galaxian 1 (Ken Wayne) & The Prince of Darkness drew Tom Prichard & The Jaguar (Danny Davis) & Tommy & Eddie Gilbert... Adrian Street beat Don Anderson... U.S. Junior Heavyweight champion Tommy Rogers beat Frankie Laine... Buddy Landel beat Dutch Mantel to win the Mid-America title... Bobby Eaton & Stagger Lee (Koko Ware) & Terry Taylor beat The Moondogs (Rex & Spot) & Jimmy Hart... Steve Keirn beat Jerry Blackwell... The Rock-n-Roll Express (Ricky Morton & Robert Gibson) beat Southern tag team champions The Grapplers (Len Denton & Tony Anthony) via DQ... Ken Patera beat Jerry Lawler to win the CWA International title... The Assassins (Don Bass & Roger Smith) beat Jerry Lawler & Austin Idol to win the CWA tag team titles.

Mr. Olympia (Jerry Stubbs) defeated Man Mountain Harris (Later known as: Black Bart) to win the Alabama title in Birmingham, AL.

In West Palm Beach, FL at the Auditorium: NWA World heavyweight champion Harley Race defeated Dusty Rhodes by DQ.

08-16-1983: Dusty Rhodes defeated NWA World heavyweight champion Harley Race by DQ in Tampa, FL.

08-17-1983: In Sunrise, FL: NWA World heavyweight champion Harley Race defeated Mike Graham.

08-18-1983: In Jacksonville, FL: NWA World heavyweight champion Harley Race defeated Dusty Rhodes.

08-20-1983: In Sarasota, FL at the Robarts Arena: NWA World heavyweight champion Harley Race defeated Barry Windham by DQ.

In San Antonio, TX: Dick Murdoch defeated Adrian Adonis to win the "undisputed" Southwest world title. The belt is held up. Then, later it was announced that Scott Casey had won a phantom match in St. Louis over Dick Murdoch for the title. Soon after, the championship was dropped.

08-21-1983: The annual NWA convention is held in Las Vegas, NV at the Dunes Hotel.

08-24-1983: The Philadelphia Arena which hosted many WWF / WWWF shows over the years is destroyed by fire.

08-25-1983: Stampede Wrestling in Vancouver, B.C., Canada: Attendance: 9,000: Andre the Giant won a battle royal... AWA World champion Nick Bockwinkel defeated David Schultz via blood stoppage... Dynamite Kid defeated Gama Singh... Bret Hart defeated Mongolian Stomper via DQ... The Cobra (George Takano) & Hiro Saito defeated Bruce Hart & Davey Boy Smith... Keith Hart defeated Scott Ferris... Jim Neidhart & Mr. Hito defeated Cuban Assassin & Cyclone Negro... Coconut Willie defeated Wolfman Kevin.

08-26-1983: Hacksaw Duggan defeats Ted DiBiase in a steel cage, loser leaves town match in Houston, TX.

In St. Louis, MO: Hulk Hogan defeated Crusher Blackwell via count out... Dick the Bruiser battled Super Destroyer (Scott Irwin) to a no contest... David Von Erich & Jerry Lawler defeated The Blackjacks (Blackjack Mulligan & Blackjack Lanza)... Barry Windham defeated Baron Von Raschke... Roger Kirby defeated Jerry Ho (substitution for Dusty Rhodes)... Bob Orton Jr. defeated George Wells... Ron Ritchie & Mark Romero defeated Sheik Abdullah & Buck Robley.

WWF: Pittsburgh, PA: Civic Arena: Attendance: 14,000: Bill Dixon pinned Jimmy Jackson... Johnny DeFazio pinned Tony Altimore... Salvatore Bellomo pinned Butcher Vachon... WWF Intercontinental champion Don Muraco defeated Jimmy Snuka via count-out... Rocky Johnson pinned Iron Mike Sharpe... Ivan Putski pinned Ivan Koloff... Andre the Giant defeated Big John Studd in a steel cage match. Swede Hanson was the guest referee.

08-27-1983: WWF in New York City, NY at Madison Square Garden. Results: Invader II (Johnny Rivera) defeated Don Kernodle... Iron Mike Sharpe defeated Swede Hanson... Chief Jay Strongbow defeated Butcher Vachon... Ivan Koloff battled Salvatore Bellomo to a time limit draw... Tiger Chung Lee defeated Tony Garea... Andre the Giant & Rocky Johnson & Ivan Putski & Tito Santana defeated Big John Studd & Sgt. Slaughter & Wild Samoans Sika & Samula... WWF Intercontinental champion Don Muraco defeated Jimmy Snuka by countout... WWF champion Bob Backlund defeated George Steele in 39 seconds.

08-28-1983: Junkyard Dog & Steve Williams defeated King Kong Bundy & Ted DiBiase in a loser-leaves town match in Tulsa, OK.

Georgia Championship Wrestling (GCW) in the Omni in Atlanta, GA. Results: Buzz Sawyer defeated Dick Slater by DQ... Pez Whatley defeated Great Kabuki... NWA World tag team champions Jack & Jerry Brisco defeated The Road Warriors (Hawk & Animal) in a Texas tornado tag team match... Tommy Rich defeated Bill Irwin in a handcuff match... Mr. Wrestling II (Johnny Walker) battled Larry Zbyszko to a double DQ... Bruno Sammartino, Jr. (David) defeated Bob Roop... Paul Ellering defeated Bruno Sammartino, Jr... Mr. Wrestling (Tim Woods) defeated Joe Lightfoot.

AWA in St. Paul, MN: Baron Von Raschke beat Chris Markoff... David Schultz beat Buck Zumhofe... Jim Brunzell beat Bill White... Ken Patera & Jerry

Blackwell beat Dino Bravo & Steve O... AWA World heavyweight champion Nick Bockwinkel beat Wahoo McDaniel... Hulk Hogan beat Mr. Saito by DQ.

08-29-1983: In Memphis, TN: Mid-South Coliseum drawing 7,743: The Jaguar (Danny Davis) beat Bruise Brother 1... Spike Huber drew Bruiser Brother 2... Dennis Condrey beat Don Anderson... Tom Prichard beat The Prince of Darkness via DQ... Koko Ware beat Buddy Landel to win the Mid-America title... The Moondogs (Rex & Spot) beat Terry Taylor & Bobby Eaton in a bone on a pole match... Jerry Lawler & Austin Idol & Jimmy Valiant beat The Assassins (Don Bass & Roger Smith) & Ken Patera in a no DQ match.

08-31-1983: WWF champion Bob Backlund appears on a Florida wrestling card in Miami, FL losing to Ron Bass by DQ.

At the Irish McNeill's Boys Club in Shreveport, LA on the Mid-South television tapings Hacksaw Duggan defeated Ted DiBiase in a no DQ loser leaves town match. On the same TV tapings The Road Warriors debut for Mid-South losing to Jim Duggan & Magnum T.A. by DQ and defeating Art Crews & Rick Rood (AKA: Rick Rude) in another match.

All-Japan Pro Wrestling: in Tokyo, Japan: **Terry Funk** Retirement Show: Sumo Hall drawing 12,000: NWA International Junior champion Chavo Guerrero pinned Masanobu Fuchi... Jumbo Tsuruta beat Bruiser Brody via countout to win the NWA International title... Terry & Dory Funk, Jr. beat Stan Hansen & Terry Gordy.

DragonKingKarl Note: I love Terry Funk. He is absolutely one of my favorite wrestlers ever. Now, mind you, he retired more times than Frank Gotch and he didn't retire here either. Still, this show was a huge success for All-Japan. Terry Funk would go on wrestling for many more years, a tremendous run for WCW in 1989 and then, famously, recreating himself as the Hardcore Legend in the 1990s for Japanese hardcore promotions and participating in death matches and then with Extreme Championship Wrestling (ECW).

September 1983

09-01-1983: In Jacksonville, FL: WWF champion Bob Backlund defeated Kareem Muhammad (Leroy Brown).

In Wichita Falls, TX: Scott Casey defeated Tully Blanchard to retain the "undisputed" Southwest World title. This is likely the last reference to this title before being dropped.

09-02-1983: The Cobra (George Takano) defeated Bruce Hart for the Stampede Commonwealth title in Calgary.

09-04-1983: Riding the incredible popularity of the CWA Memphis wrestling television show, WMC-TV debuts *The Jerry Lawler Show*, a talk show styled program hosted by Jerry Lawler

Mike Graham defeated NWA World heavyweight champion Harley Race in Orlando, FL but did not win the title.

09-05-1983: World Class Labor Day Star Wars: in Fort Worth, TX at the Convention Center drawing 11,573: Chris Adams defeated Mr. Ebony (Tom Jones)... Kerry Von Erich defeated Michael Hayes in a "country whipping" match... World Class Texas champion David Von Erich defeated Terry Gordy... Kevin Von Erich defeated World Class American champion Jimmy Garvin via DQ... Bruiser Brody defeated Kamala via DQ in a lumberjack match... Johnny Mantell defeated The Mongol (Gene Petit)... World Class World Six-Man tag team champions The Freebirds (Michael Hayes & Terry Gordy & Buddy Roberts) defeated Kerry & Kevin & David Von Erich... Iceman Parsons defeated Buddy Roberts.

In Memphis, TN: Mid-South Coliseum drawing 6,696: Bruiser Brother 2 beat Jeff Young... Bobby Fulton beat Frankie Laine... The Jaguar (Danny Davis) & The Stray Cat (Ken Wayne) & Bobby Fulton & Spike Huber beat Dream Machine (Troy Graham) & Porkchop Cash & The Prince of Darkness & Lucifer... U.S. Junior heavyweight Champ Tommy Rogers beat Carl Fergie... The Rock-n-Roll Express (Ricky Morton & Robert Gibson) beat Southern tag team champions The Grapplers (Len Denton & Tony Anthony) via DQ... Buddy Landel beat Koko Ware to win the Mid-America title. Eddie Marlin and Jimmy Hart were the special referees... Bobby Eaton & Terry Taylor & Tom Prichard beat The Moondogs (Rex & Spot) & The Giant Rebel (Stan Frazier)... CWA tag team champions The Assassins (Don Bass & Roger Smith) battled The Fabulous Ones (Steve Keirn & Stan Lane) to a double count out. As a result, the titles were held-up... Austin Idol beat Ken Patera to win the CWA International title... Bill Dundee beat Dutch Mantel... Jerry Lawler beat Bill Dundee to win the vacant Southern title.

09-06-1983: Blackjack Mulligan defeated NWA World heavyweight champion Harley Race in Tampa, FL but did not win the title.

09-07-1983: In Miami Beach, FL at the Convention Center: Attendance: 5,675: Dusty Rhodes defeated Purple Haze (Mark Lewin) in a chain match… NWA World heavyweight champion Harley Race defeated Ric Flair… Angelo Mosca & Blackjack Mulligan defeated Zambuie Express (Elijah Akeem & Kareem Muhammad) by DQ… Jos LeDuc defeated Barry Windham in a lumberjack match… Mike Graham defeated Ron Bass by DQ… Scott McGhee defeated Kevin Sullivan by DQ… Charlie Cook battled Les Thornton to a draw.

09-08-1983: In Jacksonville, FL: NWA World heavyweight champion Harley Race defeated Barry Windham.

09-09-1983: World Class TV tapings at the Sportatorium in Dallas, TX: Bruiser Brody defeated Terry Gordy… Kevin & Kerry Von Erich defeated Mongol (Gene Petit) & Mr. Ebony (Tom Jones)… Terry Gordy defeated Ken Johnson… Iceman Parsons defeated Jimmy Garvin… Chris Adams battled Buddy Roberts to a draw… Kerry Von Erich defeated Mr. Ebony… Johnny Mantell defeated Cocoa Samoa.

09-10-1983: In Lakeland, FL for the Championship Wrestling from Florida promotion Dusty Rhodes defeated Kevin Sullivan in a loser-leave town for 60 days match. Also on the show NWA World heavyweight champion Harley Race defeated Barry Windham.

WWF: Landover, MD: Capital Centre: Attendance: 15,271: Don Kernodle defeated Jeff Craney... Big John Studd defeated Salvatore Bellomo... Tiger Chung Lee defeated Pete Sanchez... Sgt. Slaughter defeated Tony Garea... The Invaders (Jose Gonzalez & Johnny Rivera) defeated Charlie Brown & Butcher Vachon... Chief Jay Strongbow fought Iron Mike Sharpe to a draw... Tito Santana defeated Ivan Koloff... SD Jones & Rocky Johnson & Tony Atlas defeated Wild Samoans (Afa & Sika & Samula)... WWF Intercontinental champion Don Muraco defeated Jimmy Snuka via count-out... WWF champion Bob Backlund defeated George Steele.

09-11-1983: At the Omni in Atlanta, GA: Junkyard Dog defeated Buzz Sawyer by DQ... No DQ: Roddy Piper & Tommy Rich defeated Bill Irwin & King Kong Bundy... Texas Death Match: Pez Whatley defeated Greg Valentine... Bruno Sammartino, Jr. defeated Larry Zbyszko... Brett Sawyer defeated Mr. Wrestling (Tim Woods).

In San Antonio, TX: Scott Casey defeated Tully Blanchard for the Southwest heavyweight title.

09-12-1983: In Memphis, TN: Mid-South Coliseum drawing 5,154: Tom Prichard drew the Jaguar (Danny Davis)... The Rock-n-Roll Express (Ricky Morton & Robert Gibson) drew Dream Machine (Troy Graham) & Porkchop Cash... U.S. Junior Heavyweight champion Tommy Rogers beat Mid-America champion Buddy Landel via DQ... Southern tag team champions The Grapplers (Len Denton & Tony Anthony) beat Dutch Mantel & Koko Ware... The Assassins (Don Bass & Roger Smith) beat The Fabulous Ones (Steve Keirn & Stan Lane) to win the held-up CWA tag team titles… The Moondogs (Rex & Spot) & Dennis Condrey battled Bobby Eaton & Bill Dundee & The Giant Rebel (Stan Frazier) to a no contest… The Assassins (Don Bass & Roger Smith) beat Bill Dundee & Big Red in a lights out match… Stan Hansen beat Austin Idol via countout to win the CWA International title… Jesse Ventura pinned Jerry Lawler to win the Southern title.

09-13-1983: Eddie Gilbert makes his first WWF TV appearance since injuring his neck in a car accident and appears with Buddy Rogers on Rogers' Corner along with WWF champion Bob Backlund. **The Iron Sheik** returns to the WWF at this TV taping defeating Bob Clement in his first match back. Rene Goulet returns to the WWF after a three year absence defeating Ray Coutu. Tonga Kid made his WWF TV debut at this show defeating Israel Matia. This TV taping also featured the Masked Superstar (Bill Eadie) "injuring" Eddie Gilbert in Gilbert's return match with multiple corkscrew neckbreakers.

DragonKingKarl Note: The first domino falls in the rise to Hulk-A-Mania and a whole new era in professional wrestling. The Iron Sheik (Hossain Khosrow Ali Vaziri) has spent most of the year in Georgia Championship Wrestling (GCW) and now comes into the WWF with Freddie Blassie (now calling himself "Ayatollah " Blassie as his manager). It is interesting that the Iron Sheik was chosen to end Bob Backlund's long reign as WWF champion. It seemed as though the obvious choice for a go-between from Bob Backlund to Hulk Hogan would have been Sgt. Slaughter who had been the top heel challenger in this era. Another name that has been often mentioned as a potential transitional champion was the Masked Superstar (Bill Eadie) and certainly that would have been fine also. However, in hindsight, with the character they were going to build with Hulk Hogan, a "say your prayers and take your vitamins' ' pro U.S.A. superhero, the Iron Sheik was a great choice.

09-16-1983: In St. Louis, MO **David Von Erich** defeated Ric Flair to win the NWA Missouri title. Also on the show Hulk Hogan defeated Jerry Blackwell.

DragonKingKarl Note: With Ric Flair slated to regain the NWA World heavyweight title from Harley Race in two months at the first Starrcade, it is only natural to build up a future challenger. David Von Erich was being seriously considered for a run with the NWA World heavyweight title at some point so winning the "Stepping stone to the NWA title" Missouri championship was a natural step in building up David Von Erich for a future World champion Ric Flair. In Puerto Rico, the WWC North American champion Pedro Morales would defeat Ric Flair as well. A similar move was made in Southeastern wrestling with Southeastern heavyweight champion Bob Armstrong successfully defending that title against Flair before Starrcade setting him up as a strong challenger in that territory as well.

09-17-1983: JCP: Charlotte, NC: Coliseum: Attendance: 5,629: Brett Hart (Barry Horowitz) defeated Jerry Grey… Scott McGhee defeated Kelly Kiniski… The Assassins (Jody Hamilton & Hercules Hernandez) defeated Ric McCord & Keith Larsen… Bob Orton Jr. defeated Johnny Weaver… Charlie Brown (Jimmy Valiant) defeated NWA TV champion Great Kabuki… Ricky Steamboat & Jay Youngblood defeated NWA World tag team champions Jack & Jerry Brisco but did not win the titles.

Bob Armstrong turns babyface following an exceptional heel run in SECW when he is attacked by the Midnight Express (Ron Starr & Norvell Austin & Randy Rose) and given a piledriver on the concrete in retaliation for Bob taking up for his sons Scott & Steve Armstrong.

Barry Windham defeated Jos LeDuc in Sarasota, FL to win the Florida title.

WWC: 10th Anniversary Show: in San Juan, PR: Hiram Bithorn Stadium drawing 27,000: Miguel Perez pinned Barabbas… Pete Sanchez beat Assassin 2… Bob Sweetan pinned Gama Singh… Hercules Ayala pinned The Iron Sheik… Pierre Martel pinned Don Kent… Abdullah Tomba pinned **Gorilla Monsoon**… WWC & Caribbean tag team champions The Super Medics (Jose Estrada & Johnny Rodz) beat Chief Thundercloud & Chuy… WWC North American champion Pedro Morales beat Ric Flair via DQ… WWC Puerto Rican champion King Tonga (Meng/Haku) pinned Dory Funk, Jr… Invader 2 (Roberto Soto) pinned Ox Baker… Kendo Nagasaki drew El Gran Apollo… WWC Universal champion Carlos Colon drew NWA World champion Harley Race… Mil Mascaras & Dos Caras beat The Infernos (Tim Tall Tree & Gypsy Joe)… Andre the Giant beat Abdullah the Butcher via countout.

DragonKingKarl Note: Why was WWF talent Gorilla Monsoon and the Iron Sheik wrestling on this World Wrestling Council (WWC) show in San Juan, Puerto Rico? Because Gorilla Monsoon was part owner of the promotion, and oftentimes worked with the WWF more freely than other territories.

09-18-1983: Jos LeDuc regains the Florida title from Barry Windham in Orlando, FL.

09-19-1983: In Memphis, TN at the Mid-South Coliseum in front of 4,618 fans The Assassins (Roger Smith & Don Bass) lost the CWA tag team titles to The Fabulous Ones (Steve Keirn & Stan Lane). Also on the show Dutch Mantel & Koko Ware defeated The Grapplers (Len Denton & Tony Anthony) for the Southern tag team titles.

09-20-1983: In Tampa, FL at the Ft. Hesterly Armory a big show takes place with a main event of a steel cage, loser leaves town for one year match. Dusty Rhodes defeats Lucifer and unmasks him as Kevin Sullivan. Also on card: Barry Windham defeated Southern heavyweight champion Ron Bass by DQ... Angelo Mosca went to a double countout with Jos LeDuc... Mike Rotundo defeated The Purple Haze (Mark Lewin)... Zambuie Express (Ray Candy & Leroy Brown AKA: Elijah Akeem & Kareem Muhammad) defeated Hector Guerrero & Mike Davis... Sam Houston defeated Mike Fever.

09-23-1983: WWF Intercontinental champion Don Muraco defeated WWF champion Bob Backlund by count out in White Plains, NY.

In Houston, TX Junkyard Dog defeated AWA World heavyweight champion Nick Bockwinkel in a non-title match.

Saga of the Death of David Von Erich: World Class Championship Wrestling TV taping at the Sportatorium in Dallas, TX: Terry Gordy defeated Kerry Von Erich by DQ... Bruiser Brody defeated Michael Hayes by DQ... David Von Erich & Chris

Adams defeated Mongol (Gene Petit) & Boris Zhukov by DQ... Johnny Mantell battled Buddy Roberts to a draw... Johnny Mantell defeated Bill Rathke... David Von Erich defeated Mongol... Iceman Parsons defeated Bill Rathke.

EMLL: 50th Anniversary Show; in Mexico City, Mexico: Arena Mexico drawing 18,000: Mexican National Middleweight champion Ultraman beat El Supremo... Kevin Von Erich & Mascara Año 2000 & Halcon Ortiz beat Herodes & Coloso Colosetti & Pirata Morgan... Ringo Mendoza & Villano III & Lizmark beat Fiera & Mocho Cota & Espectro Jr... Sangre Chicana beat MS-1 in a hair vs. hair match.

09-24-1983: Mike Rotundo defeated Ron Bass for the Southern (FL) heavyweight title in St. Petersburg, FL.

WWF: Philadelphia, PA: Spectrum: Attendance: 18,983: Televised on the PRISM Network: Salvatore Bellomo defeated Butcher Vachon... Don Kernodle defeated Israel Matia... The Invaders (Jose Gonzalez & Johnny Rivera) defeated Swede Hanson & Iron Mike Sharpe via count-out... WWF Intercontinental champion Don Muraco pinned Chief Jay Strongbow... WWF champion Bob Backlund pinned Sgt. Slaughter in a Texas Death Match... Andre the Giant defeated Big John Studd in a steel cage match... Tiger Chung Lee defeated Rene Goulet... Penny Mitchell & Susan Starr defeated Judy Martin & Fabulous Moolah... Jimmy Snuka & Tito Santana & Rocky Johnson defeated Ivan Koloff & the Wild Samoans (Afa & Sika).

09-25-1983: AWA: St. Paul, MN: Attendance: 15,762: Brad Rheingans battled AWA World heavyweight champion Nick Bockwinkel to a draw. On the same show: Hulk Hogan defeated David Schultz & Mr. Saito by DQ in a handicap match... The Highfliers (Greg Gagne & Jim Brunzell) & Rick Martel defeated Ken Patera & Jerry Blackwell & Sheik Adnan... Blackjack Lanza defeated Bobby Heenan... Buck Zumhofe defeated Steve Regal... Steve O battled Bill White to a draw.

GCW at the Omni in Atlanta, GA Brett Wayne (Sawyer) defeated Larry Zbyszko to win the NWA National title in front of 3,500 fans.

09-26-1983: Bob Armstrong defeated Ric Flair to retain the NWA Southeastern title in Birmingham, AL.

In West Palm Beach, FL: NWA World heavyweight champion Harley Race defeated Barry Windham by count out.

In San Antonio, TX: The Fabulous Blondes (Eric Embry & Ken Timbs) defeated Scott Casey & Buddy Moreno to win the Southwest tag team titles. Scott Casey was substituting for Bobby Jaggers.

09-28-1983: Barry Windham defeated NWA World heavyweight champion Harley Race by DQ in Miami Beach, FL.

09-29-1983: Blackjack Mulligan defeated NWA World heavyweight champion Harley Race by DQ in Jacksonville, FL.

October 1983

10-01-1983: Wayne Farris (AKA: Honky Tonk Man) joins Randy Rose & Ron Starr as a member of the Midnight Express when he defeats Bob Armstrong on television in Dothan, AL and Rose & Starr run in to assist him.

In St. Petersburg, FL at the Bayfront Center: NWA World heavyweight champion Harley Race battled Dusty Rhodes to a double count out.

In San Antonio, TX: Ralampago Leon defeated Eric Embry to the Southwest Junior heavyweight title.

DragonKingKarl Note: The "Saga of the Death of David Von Erich (David Adkisson)" is noted several times throughout this book. This refers to a special podcast series from *When It Was Cool Wrestling* Podcast (available on all major podcast apps and directly from WhenItWasCool.com) by Karl Stern detailing the last several months of David Von Erich's life leading up to his death in 1984. Whenever the "Saga of the Death of David Von Erich" is mentioned it is a reference point for that podcast series. There has been much myth, incorrect information, and speculation about the death of David Von Erich. Everything from speculation about an injury as far back as October of 1983 to drug use to a medical emergency. This podcast series dug up literally every single detail I could find about David Von Erich in the months leading up to his death. Some of these "Saga of the Death of David Von Erich" notes may seem trivial but they are included due to speculation about the months leading up to his death. I include them here and on the When It Was Cool website as a way for researchers and historians to have the facts at their fingertips, without conjecture or speculation, when writing or researching his death.

Saga of the Death of David Von Erich - World Class television show: Video of NWA World heavyweight champion Harley Race verses Kevin Von Erich from June 10, 1983. Kevin's arm is "injured" during the match. David Von Erich comes down to ringside to cheer on Kevin but Harley kicks David and David attacks Race causing a DQ. David beats down Race and throws the NWA title belt down on top of him. David vows to quit wrestling if he doesn't beat Race (or Flair). The show then re-airs the "Valet for a Day " feature where Jimmy Garvin and Sunshine had to work for David for a day on the ranch. The Mongol (Gene Petit) managed by Skandar Akbar verses David Von Erich. Referee Bronco Lubich. David wins with the Iron Claw. The Mongol blades. David looks energetic and quick in the match. Hitting several high drop kicks and a flying knee.

10-03-1983: Ricky Steamboat & Jay Youngblood win the NWA World tag team championship from Jack & Jerry Brisco in Greenville, SC.

At the Mid-South Coliseum in Memphis, TN in front of 6,619 fans Jerry Lawler defeated Jesse Ventura managed by Jimmy Hart to win the Southern title. On the same show Austin Idol defeated Stan Hansen to regain the International title. Porkchop Cash & Dream Machine (managed by Jimmy Hart) defeated Dutch Mantel & Koko Ware to win the Southern tag team titles and, in what may have been the first ever meeting between the **Rock & Roll Express** (Ricky Morton & Robert Gibson) and a version of the Midnight Express, the Rock & Roll Express defeated **The Midnight Express** (Dennis Condrey & Norvell Austin).

DragonKingKarl Note: The feud between the Rock & Roll Express and Midnight Express spanned multiple territories and was considered the gold standard for tag team wrestling for decades. This may have been their first meeting. While Norvell Austin would be replaced by Bobby Eaton when they moved to Mid-South, the Dennis Condrey & Norvell Austin pairing had a lot of experience and history behind them at this point. The Rock & Roll Express would face many versions of the Midnight Express over the years: Dennis Condrey & Norvell Austin, Dennis Condrey & Bobby Eaton, Bobby Eaton & Stan Lane, and even the much ridiculed New Midnight Express of Bob Holly & Bart Gunn (yes, they actually met on an independent show in Memphis, TN June 23, 1998!)

10-04-1983: In Tampa, FL: NWA World heavyweight champion Harley Race battled Dusty Rhodes to a double DQ.

UWA Mexico: in Mexico City, Mexico: Palacio de los Deportes drawing 28,000: UWA Heavyweight champion El Canek beat Dos Caras.

10-07-1983: WWF: Pittsburgh, PA: Civic Arena: Attendance: 12,000: Pat Patterson pinned Samula... Rocky Johnson fought Sika to a draw... Afa defeated Ivan Putski via count-out... Tito Santana pinned Iron Mike Sharpe... Tony Garea defeated Bill Dixon... Tiger Chung Lee pinned Jimmy Jackson... Susan Starr & Penny Mitchell defeated Fabulous Moolah & Judy Martin... WWF Intercontinental champion Don Muraco defeated Jimmy Snuka via DQ.

World Class TV taping at the Sportatorium in Dallas, TX: NWA World Heavyweight champion Harley Race defeated Iceman Parsons by DQ... David Von Erich defeated Jimmy Garvin by DQ... Michael Hayes defeated Johnny Mantell... Kamala defeated Art Crews... Chris Adams & Johnny Mantell defeated Michael

Hayes & Buddy Roberts... Jose Lothario defeated Mongol (Gene Petit) by DQ... Jimmy Garvin defeated Art Crews... Boris Zhukov (Jim Nelson) defeated Mike Reed.

10-08-1983: Hulk Hogan defeated NWA World heavyweight champion Harley Race by DQ when Hogan was thrown over the top rope in a match in St. Louis, MO at the Kiel Auditorium. Attendance 6,000.

WWF: Boston, MA: Boston Garden: Attendance: 15,550: Rene Goulet defeated Rudy Diamond... Israel Matia defeated Chuck Tanner... The Tonga Kid defeated Fred Marzino... The Invaders (Jose Gonzalez & Johnny Rivera) defeated Pete Doherty & Butcher Vachon... The Masked Superstar (Bill Eadie) defeated WWF champion Bob Backlund via count-out... SD Jones defeated Bob Bradley... Chief Jay Strongbow defeated Don Kernodle... Sgt. Slaughter defeated Swede Hanson... WWF Intercontinental champion Don Muraco defeated Jimmy Snuka in a steel cage match.

Central States: St. Louis, MO: Attendance: 6,000: Ron Ritchie & Bob Brown & Angelo Mosca Jr. defeated Roger Kirby & Jerry Brown & Sheik Abdullah... Buck Robley defeated Jerry Ho... Iceman King Parsons defeated Tonga John (The Barbarian)... Blackjack Mulligan defeated Buzz Tyler... Barry Windham & David Von Erich defeated Jerry Blackwell & Super Destroyer (Scott Irwin)... Hulk Hogan defeated NWA World champion Harley Race via disqualification.

Saga of the Death of David Von Erich - World Class television show: The Mongol (Gene Petit) & Boris Zhukoff (Jim Nelson) (managed by Skandor Akbar) verses David Von Erich & Chris Adams. Referee: Jerry Usher. Chris Adams & David Von Erich win when Skandor Akbar interferes. David puts the claw on Akbar. Slow, plodding, low energy match. David Von Erich hits a nice flying head scissors early on. Main event is Terry Gordy verses Kerry Von Erich. Gordy continues to beat on Kerry late in the match and David runs in and saves Kerry and puts the claw on Gordy. Terry Gordy wins by DQ.

10-09-1983: Blackjack Mulligan defeated Kareem Muhammad for the Florida Brass Knuckles title in Orlando, FL. Also, Barry Windham defeated NWA World heavyweight champion Harley Race by DQ.

10-10-1983: At the Mid-South Coliseum in Memphis, TN Jesse Ventura defeated Jerry Lawler to regain the Southern title in a no DQ match. Andy Kauffman returns dressed in a chicken suit. Koko Ware defeated Tommy Rogers for the U.S. Junior title, this is a different title than the Ron Fuller Southeastern U.S. Junior title where Tim Horner is champion at this time. Attendance was 4,324.

10-12-1983: Ernie Roth, AKA: The Grand Wizard who has been managing in the WWF dies of a heart attack at age 54.

At the Irish McNeill's Boys Club in Shreveport, LA on Mid-South television Jim Duggan & Magnum T.A. lost the Mid-South tag team titles to Jim Neidhart & Butch Reed.

10-13-1983: Hulk Hogan fought NWA World heavyweight champion Harley Race to a no contest in Kansas City, MO.

10-15-1983: Saga of the Death of David Von Erich - World Class television show: Main event is Jimmy Garvin (with both Sunshine & Precious) verses David Von Erich. Referee: Bronko Lubich. David is energetic and entertaining during the match. Kamala runs in and attacks David. David wins by DQ. David puts the Iron Claw on Kamala and Jimmy Garvin bails out.

10-16-1983: Don Kernodle defeated Mike Rotundo to win the Canadian TV title in Toronto, Canada at the Maple Leaf Gardens.

JCP: Greensboro, NC: Coliseum: Attendance: 5,229: Terry Gibbs defeated Tom Lintz… Gene Anderson defeated Keith Larsen… Scott McGhee defeated Magic Dragon… Wahoo McDaniel defeated Dick Slater via DQ… Dory Funk Jr. & Bugsy McGraw & Mark Youngblood defeated Paul Jones & The Assassins (Jody Hamilton & Hercules Hernandez)… Jack & Jerry Brisco defeated NWA World tag team champions Ricky Steamboat & Jay Youngblood via DQ… Charlie Brown (Jimmy Valiant) pinned Baron Von Raschke in a steel cage match… Ric Flair pinned Bob Orton Jr. in a steel cage match.

10-17-1983: WWF in New York City, NY at Madison Square Garden. Attendance: 22,092 with several thousand watching on closed-circuit at the Felt Forum. Results: Tony Garea defeated Rene Goulet… Tiger Chung Lee, managed by Freddie Blassie defeated SD Jones… Sgt. Slaughter defeated Ivan Putski by DQ… Masked Superstar (Bill Eadie) defeated WWF champion Bob Backlund by countout… Mike Graham defeated Bob Bradley… WWF Intercontinental champion Don Muraco defeated Jimmy Snuka in a steel cage match after being knocked out of the door. Following the match Jimmy Snuka climbed to the top of the steel cage to hit the Superfly Splash off the top in this famous moment in wrestling history… Rocky Johnson defeated Wild Samoan Sika… The Invaders (Jose Gonzalez & Johnny Rivera) defeated Israel Matia & Butcher Vachon… Andre the Giant defeated Wild Samoan Afa… The Invaders defeated Rene Goulet & Don Kernodle.

In Memphis, TN: Mid-South Coliseum drawing 7,288: Bobby Fulton beat Robert Reed… The Russian Invader (Jerry Novak) beat The Jaguar (Danny Davis)… Princess Victoria beat Judy Martin… Jimmy Hart & Jim Cornette beat Bobby Eaton in a handicap match… Tommy Rogers beat Koko Ware to win the U.S. Junior Heavyweight title… Jerry Lawler & Austin Idol beat **The Assassins (Don Bass & Roger Smith)**… Jesse Ventura beat Jimmy Valiant via DQ… Jesse Ventura & The Midnight Express (Dennis Condrey & Norvell Austin) & Buddy Landel & The Assassins (Don Bass & Roger Smith) beat Jerry Lawler & Roughhouse Fargo & Jimmy Valiant & Austin Idol & The Fabulous Ones (Steve Keirn & Stan Lane) in a hospital elimination match.

DragonKingKarl Note: Don Bass and Roger Smith are unsung heroes of wrestling in Memphis. They must have had a least a dozen different gimmicks between the two of them and often teamed up as a tag team. Do you need a brute brawling tag team? Then call Don Bass and Roger Smith. Just a few of the gimmicks they had collectively or individually in Memphis include: The Assassins, The A-Team, The New York Assassins, Dirty Rhodes, The Singing Cowboy, Fire & Flame, many others.

10-19-1983: Andre the Giant loaned to the AWA for a series of dates starting with Dauphin, Manitoba, Canada where he teamed with Rick Martel to defeat the AWA World tag team champions Ken Patera & Jerry Blackwell in a non-title match.

10-20-1983: In Winnipeg, Canada: Attendance: 10,036: Andre the Giant & Rick Martel & Mad Dog Vachon defeated Ken Patera & Jerry Blackwell & Sheik Adnan Al Kassie. On the same show Hulk Hogan battled David Schultz to a no contest and Jim Brunzell defeated Superstar Billy Graham.

10-21-1983: Jack & Jerry Brisco defeated Ricky Steamboat & Jay Youngblood to win the NWA World tag team titles in Richmond, VA.

In Denver, CO Andre the Giant won a 20 man battle royal on an AWA show and teamed with Mad Dog Vachon & Rick Martel to defeat Superstar Billy Graham & Mr. Saito & David Schultz.

World Class TV tapings at the Sportatorium in Dallas, TX: Chris Adams & Johnny Mantell defeated The Freebirds (Michael Hayes & Terry Gordy)… Kevin Von Erich defeated Terry Gordy by reversed decision… Junkyard Dog battled Kamala to a double DQ… Michael Hayes defeated Jose Lothario… Princess Victoria defeated Judy Martin… Masked Avenger (Chris Adams) defeated Jimmy Garvin… Black Gordman defeated Mike Reed… Johnny Mantell defeated Mr. Ebony (Tom Jones).

In St. Louis, MO: St. Louis, MO: Hulk Hogan defeated Crusher Blackwell in a steel cage match… NWA Missouri champion David Von Erich defeated Super Destroyer (Scott Irwin)… Dick the Bruiser & Jimmy Snuka defeated Blackjack

Mulligan & Killer Karl Krupp... Jimmy Snuka (substituting for Barry Windham) defeated Roger Kirby... Iceman Parsons defeated Doug Sommers... Buck Robley defeated **Booker T** (Bubba Douglas)... Bulldog Bob Brown & Angelo Mosca Jr defeated Jerry Brown & Tonga John (The Barbarian).

DragonKingKarl Note: Yes, years before Booker T. Huffman, Jr. wrestled as the famous "Booker T", there was briefly a Booker T in wrestling: Bubba Douglas. Andrew "Bubba" Douglas wrestled in multiple promotions, most famously in Florida. He died at the age of 42 in 1986 from a heart attack.

10-22-1983: Saga of the Death of David Von Erich - World Class wrestling TV: Replay of David Von Erich putting the Iron Claw on Kamala from last week. Main Event: NWA World heavyweight champion Harley Race verses Iceman King Parsons. David Von Erich is in the ring for the introduction. Race protests David Manning as referee and David Von Erich being at ringside. Harley slaps David from the inside of the ring. David hits Harley which gets Iceman Parsons disqualified.

AWA: San Francisco, CA: Cow Palace: Attendance 10,300: Steve O defeats Chris Markoff... Ray Stevens defeats Bill White... Mr. Saito defeats Baron Von Raschke... Blackjack Lanza defeats Bobby Heenan by Count Out... Hulk Hogan defeats David Schultz... Andre the Giant & Mad Dog Vachon & Rick Martel defeat Sheik Adnan Al-Kassie & The Sheiks (Jerry Blackwell & Ken Patera)... 16 Man Battle Royal: Mad Dog Vachon wins. Also in the match: Andre The Giant, Baron Von Raschke, Bill White, Blackjack Lanza, Bobby Heenan, Chris Markoff,

David Schultz, Hulk Hogan, Jerry Blackwell, Ken Patera, Mr. Saito, Ray Stevens, Rick Martel, Sheik Adnan Al-Kassie, and Steve O.

10-23-1983: 19,000 fans turn out in St. Paul, MN to see the following AWA show: Mad Dog Vachon won a 20 man battle royal… Hulk Hogan battled Mr. Saito to a no contest… Mad Dog Vachon & Rick Martel defeated AWA World tag team champions Ken Patera & Jerry Blackwell in a non-title match… Otto Wanz defeated Bill White… Blackjack Lanza & Ray Stevens defeated Bobby Heenan & Mr. Saito… Billy Robinson defeated Chris Markoff.

The Last Battle of Atlanta show takes place for Georgia Championship Wrestling at the Omni in front of 10,600 people. Results: In a lights out match Ole Anderson defeated Paul Ellering… In a steel cage match Tommy Rich defeated Buzz Sawyer… Jimmy Valiant & Pez Whatley battled The Road Warriors (Hawk & Animal) to a double DQ for the National tag team titles… Jake Roberts battled Brett Wayne (Sawyer) to a no contest over the National heavyweight title… Mr. Wrestling II (Johnny Walker) defeated Bob Roop… Great Kabuki defeated NWA National TV champion Ronnie Garvin but did not win the title due to time limit… Les Thornton defeated Joe Lightfoot… Bruno Sammartino, Jr. (David Sammartino) defeated Pat Rose.

DragonKingKarl Note: This show gained an almost mythological reputation over the years, largely due to the film being lost for a long time. The only thing wrestling fans knew, beyond the 10,600 people who were there and saw it first hand, was from the coverage in the newsstand magazines, most notably the photos and story by Bill Apter. The photos and story made it look like it was a war. The uniqueness (at the time) of a steel cage with a roof added to the story. Both Tommy Rich and Buzz Sawyer bled buckets. As the years passed the story grew. During the tape trading era of the 1990s this was the Holy Grail of video tapes and nobody had it or could find it. It was feared forever lost and old school wrestling fans and historians longed to see it. Strangely enough, the film showed up in the archives of WWE who had purchased all of the Georgia Championship Wrestling footage on an unmarked reel of house show tape. While manually going through it, one of the WWE Network employees realized what was there and, finally, in September of 2016 the match was uploaded to the WWE Network amid great fanfare. I even appeared on multiple podcasts to discuss it. The match, sadly, was unexceptional really for a cage match. It was basically every cage match you have seen from the era. Without the context of the story The Last Battle of Atlanta steel cage match between Tommy Rich and Buzz Sawyer lost a lot of its luster.

10-24-1983: NWA World heavyweight champion Harley Race begins a tour of Japan and defeats Jumbo Tsuruta in his first match in Kitami, Japan.

Tim Horner defeated Chick Donovan for the NWA U.S. Junior title in a loser leave town match in Birmingham, AL.

The Assassins (Roger Smith & Don Bass) defeated The Fabulous Ones (Steve Keirn & Stan Lane) for the CWA tag team titles at the Mid-South Coliseum in Memphis, TN. Attendance 3,915.

10-26-1983: NWA World heavyweight champion Harley Race battles Jumbo Tsuruta to a draw in Morioka, Japan.

10-28-1983: AWA: Salt Lake City, UT: Salt Palace: Attendance 10,640: Jim Brunzell defeats Bill White… Billy Robinson defeats Ray Stevens… Blackjack Lanza defeats Bobby Heenan… Mad Dog Vachon & Rick Martel defeat The Sheiks (Jerry Blackwell & Ken Patera)… David Schultz wrestled Hulk Hogan to a No Contest… 20 Man Battle Royal: Rick Martel wins over Andre The Giant, Baron Von Raschke, Bill White, Billy Robinson, Blackjack Lanza, Bobby Heenan, Brad Rheingans, David Schultz, Greg Gagne, Hulk Hogan, Jerry Blackwell, Jim Brunzell, Ken Patera, Mad Dog Vachon, Otto Wanz, Ray Stevens, Sheik Adnan Al-Kassie, and Superstar Billy Graham.

10-29-1983: On CWA Championship Wrestling on WMC-5 in Memphis a big upset takes place as Ken Raper & Robert Reed, two TV enhancement wrestlers, defeat The Assassins (Roger Smith & Don Bass) for the CWA tag team titles.

Saga of the Death of David Von Erich - World Class wrestling TV: Highlights begin the show of a six-man tag team match: Iceman Parsons & Chris Adams & David Von Erich verses Kamala & The Mongol (Gene Petit) & Michael Hayes with Skandar Akbar at ringside. Late in the match Kamala is afraid of David Von Erich and runs from the Iron Claw. Chris Adams pins the Mongol to win following a superkick.

10-31-1983: NWA World heavyweight champion Harley Race defeats Ted DiBiase in Wakamatsu, Japan.

The Assassins (Roger Smith & Don Bass) defeat Ken Raper & Robert Reed to regain the CWA tag team titles at the Mid-South Coliseum in Memphis, TN. Then,

CWA tag team champions The Assassins battled The Fabulous Ones (Steve Keirn & Stan Lane) to a no contest. As a result, the titles were held-up. The attendance was 3,906.

November 1983

11-01-1983: WWF Intercontinental champion Don Muraco defeated WWF champion Bob Backlund by countout in Buffalo, NY.

11-03-1983: New Japan Pro Wrestling: in Tokyo, Japan: Sumo Hall drawing 13,000: Gran Hamada beat Black Cat... Big John Studd & Steven Wright beat Ryuma Go & Osamu Kido... Kuniaki Kobayashi & Isamu Teranishi beat Kazuo Yamazaki & Nobuhiko Takada... Paul Orndorff beat Masanobu Kurisu... The Cobra (George Takano) pinned Davey Boy Smith to win the vacant NWA World Junior Heavyweight title... Animal Hamaguchi beat Seiji Sakaguchi via DQ... Riki Choshu beat Akira Maeda... WWF International champion Tatsumi Fujinami battled Killer Khan to a double count out... Antonio Inoki pinned Yoshiaki Yatsu.

11-04-1983: 18,500 fans see an AWA card in Rosemont, IL: Jim Brunzell won a 20 man battle royal... Hulk Hogan & The Highfliers (Greg Gagne & Jim Brunzell) defeated Ken Patera & Jerry Blackwell & Sheik Adnan... Baron Von Raschke defeated David Schultz by DQ... Blackjack Lanza defeated Bobby Heenan... Billy Robinson defeated Bill White... Superstar Billy Graham defeated Rick Martel... Brad Rheingans defeated Chris Markoff.

World Class TV taping at the Sportatorium in Dallas, TX: Kevin & Kerry Von Erich defeated The Freebirds (Terry Gordy & Michael Hayes) by DQ in a country whipping match... Chris Adams defeated Buddy Roberts... Iceman Parsons defeated Tonga John (The Barbarians)... Chris Adams & Johnny Mantell defeated Buddy Roberts & Jimmy Garvin... Jose Lothario defeated Tonga John... Super Destroyer 1 (Scott Irwin) defeated Iceman Parsons... Super Destroyer 2 (Bill Irwin) defeated Mike Reed.

In St. Louis, MO: NWA Missouri champion David Von Erich defeated Ric Flair... Dick the Bruiser defeated Scott Farris (substituting for Blackjack Mulligan)... Barry Windham defeated Killer Karl Krupp... King Kong Brody defeated The Mongol (Gene Petit)... Velvet McIntyre & Penny Mitchell defeated Leilani Kai & Peggy Lee... Buck Robley defeated Doug Sommers... Ron Ritchie defeated Roger Kirby (substituting for Buddy Landel)... Bulldog Bob Brown & Angelo Mosca Jr defeated Scott Farris & Sheik Abdullah.

Saga of the Death of David Von Erich: Just weeks before Ric Flair is scheduled to regain the NWA World heavyweight title for the second time from Harley Race, NWA Missouri champion David Von Erich gets a big win over Ric Flair, setting him up as a top contender after Flair gets the championship. This further adds evidence to the "David Von Erich being prepped to be world champion" story had he not passed away at the age of 25 in 1984.

11-05-1983: Dusty Rhodes & Blackjack Mulligan defeated The Zambuie Express to win the United States tag team titles in Lakeland, FL.

WWF: Boston, MA: Boston Garden: Attendance 10,676: Salvatore Bellomo defeats Rudy Diamond... Charlie Fulton defeats Bob Bradley... Rene Goulet defeats Butcher Vachon... The Iron Sheik defeats Chief Jay Strongbow... Mr. Fuji & Tiger Chung Lee defeat SD Jones & Swede Hanson... WWF champion Bob Backlund wrestled The Masked Superstar (Bill Eadie) to a double count out... Tony Garea defeats Don Kernodle... Rocky Johnson defeats George Steele... Jimmy Snuka & The Invaders (Jose Gonzalez & Johnny Rivera) defeat The Wild Samoans (Afa & Samula & Sika)

11-06-1983: GCW at the Omni in Atlanta, GA: Jake Roberts defeated Ronnie Garvin to win the National TV title... The Road Warriors (Hawk & Animal) battled Dusty Rhodes & Brett Wayne Sawyer to a double DQ... Tommy Rich defeated Ted DiBiase by DQ... Jimmy Valiant defeated Great Kabuki... Buzz Sawyer battled Abdullah the Butcher to a double DQ.

11-07-1983: Super Olympia (Arn Anderson) unmasks Mr. Olympia (Jerry Stubbs) in a match in Birmingham, AL.

Bill Dundee defeated Tommy Rogers for the U.S. Junior title at the Mid-South Coliseum in Memphis, TN. Also on the show The Fabulous Ones (Steve Keirn & Stan Lane) defeated The Assassins (Roger Smith & Don Bass) for the held up CWA tag team titles and to win the masks of the Assassins. Attendance was 4,605.

11-11-1983: In Denver, CO Andre the Giant defeated AWA World champion Nick Bockwinkel by DQ.

11-12-1983: Saga of the Death of David Von Erich - World Class wrestling TV: Lengthy mid-show sit down interview with Fritz Von Erich. Kerry Von Erich presents a ring jacket to Mike Von Erich who is about to debut. Michael Hayes comes out and taunts a nervous Mike Von Erich. Hayes tears up the jacket and Mike attacks Hayes. This leads to a brawl between Mike & Kerry and Michael Hayes & Buddy Roberts. This leads to a loser leaves town match challenge between Michael Hayes and Kerry Von Erich. The main event of the show is Kerry & Kevin Von Erich verses Michael Hayes & Terry Gordy in a country whipping match. Kevin & Kerry Von Erich win by DQ due to Kevin being thrown over the top rope. David Von Erich is not on the show, nor even mentioned.

11-13-1983: Rick Martel defeated AWA World champion Nick Bockwinkel by DQ in Salt Lake City, UT. On the same show Hulk Hogan & Andre the Giant defeated Mr. Saito & David Schultz & Jerry Blackwell in a handicap match.

Toronto, Canada: Maple Leaf Gardens: Attendance 13,224: Bob Marcus defeats Tim Gerrard… Nick DeCarlo defeats Scrap Iron Sheppard… Leo Burke defeats Herb Gallant… The Destroyer (Dick Beyer) & Kurt Von Hess defeats Johnny Weaver & Billy Red Lyons… Angelo Mosca & Jimmy Valiant defeat Leo Burke & The Destroyer (Dick Beyer)… Blackjack Mulligan wrestled Masked Superstar (Bill Eadie) to a double count out… Roddy Piper defeated NWA United States champion Greg Valentine by DQ.

11-14-1983: At the Mid-South Coliseum in Memphis, TN The Rock & Roll Express (Ricky Morton & Robert Gibson) lost the Southern tag team titles to The Bruiser Brothers (Porkchop Cash & Dream Machine). On the same show The Fabulous Ones (Steve Keirn & Stan Lane) lost the CWA tag team titles to the Midnight Express (Norvell Austin & Dennis Condrey) managed by **Jim Cornette**. Attendance is 3,800.

DragonKingKarl Note: Yes, it is a little known fact that Jim Cornette briefly managed an original Midnight Express combination prior to the Dennis Condrey & Bobby Eaton line up. Here in November in Memphis he is managing Dennis Condrey & Norvell Austin. Randy Rose appeared only sporadically on these shows at this point.

In West Palm Beach, FL: NWA World heavyweight champion Harley Race defeated Dusty Rhodes in a Texas Death Match.

11-15-1983: In Tampa, FL at the Sun Dome: NWA World heavyweight champion Harley Race defeated Mike Rotundo.

Paul Orndorff makes his WWF debut in Allentown, PA defeating Mark Mattox. On this same show Tony Atlas & Rocky Johnson defeated the Wild Samoans (Afa & Sika) to win the WWF tag team titles.

DragonKingKarl Note: Another domino falls in the explosion in popularity that WWF would experience over the next few years. Paul Orndorff would be brought in as the arrogant "Mr. Wonderful" character. After Hulk Hogan wins the WWF heavyweight championship from the Iron Sheik in January 1984, Paul Orndorff would have the most lucrative run against Hulk Hogan of any opponent. While it is often "Rowdy" Roddy Piper who gets thought of as Hulk Hogan's most successful opponent of the era (and he was massively important to the WWF national expansion), in terms of house show money drawn, nobody could match Paul Orndorff.

11-16-1983: In Miami Beach, FL at the Convention Center: NWA World heavyweight champion Harley Race defeated Mike Rotundo by DQ.

11-18-1983: WWF: Pittsburgh, PA: Civic Arena: Attendance: 10,000: Salvatore Bellomo pinned Butcher Vachon... Wild Samoans (Afa & Sika) & Samula defeated SD Jones & Rocky Johnson & Tony Atlas... Eddie Gilbert pinned Bill Berger... Tito Santana pinned Don Kernodle... The Masked Superstar (Bill Eadie) defeated WWF champion Bob Backlund via count-out... The Iron Sheik pinned Tony Garea... Rene Goulet pinned Steve Lombardi... Pat Patterson defeated Ivan Koloff via count-out.

11-19-1983: Mid-South in New Orleans, LA: The Superdome drawing 8,000: Dusty Rhodes battled Nikolai Volkoff to a double count out... Kerry Von Erich pinned Missing Link... David Von Erich beat Kamala via countout.... The Road Warriors (Hawk & Animal) beat Mr. Wrestling II (Johnny Walker) & Magnum TA... Mid-South North American champion Junkyard Dog beat Butch Reed.

In St. Petersburg, FL at the Bayfront Center: NWA World heavyweight champion Harley Race defeated Ron Bass by DQ.

Saga of the Death of David Von Erich - World Class wrestling TV: The focus is back on David Von Erich for just a moment as they show David Von Erich verses Kamala highlights. David won when Friday threw in the towel for Kamala while Kamala was in the Iron Claw. Otherwise, David does not appear on the show and the main focus is on Kerry Von Erich and The Freebirds feud.

WWF: Baltimore, MD: Civic Center - Attendance: 14,000: Bob Bradley defeated Israel Matia... The Invaders (Jose Gonzalez & Johnny Rivera) defeated Don Kernodle & Charlie Fulton... Tito Santana defeated Iron Mike Sharpe... Mr. Fuji defeated Salvatore Bellomo... The Iron Sheik defeated Chief Jay Strongbow... Tony Atlas defeated Big John Studd via DQ... Jimmy Snuka defeated WWF Intercontinental champion Don Muraco via count-out... Rocky Johnson defeated Sgt. Slaughter in a steel cage match.

11-20-1983: On a show in Chicago, IL Jim Brunzell defeated AWA World heavyweight champion Nick Bockwinkel by DQ.

11-21-1983: WWF in New York City, NY at Madison Square Garden. Results: Salvatore Bellomo defeated Butcher Vachon... Tito Santana defeated Don Kernodle... WWF Intercontinental champion Don Muraco defeated Iron Mike Sharpe... The Invaders (Jose Gonzalez & Johnny Rivera) defeated Mr. Fuji & Rene Goulet... The Wild Samoans (Afa & Sika) defeated Rocky Johnson & SD Jones. The Samoans were still recognized as WWF tag team champions on this card as their title loss to Rocky Johnson & Tony Atlas had not yet aired on TV... Iron Sheik defeated Tony Garea... Tony Atlas defeated Big John Studd... Jimmy Snuka battled Sgt. Slaughter to a time limit draw... Pat Patterson defeated Ivan Koloff by countout... WWF champion Bob Backlund defeated the Masked Superstar (Bill Eadie).

At the Mid-South Coliseum in Memphis, TN Jerry Lawler defeated Andy Kaufman in a boxing match with Jimmy Hart in the corner of Kaufman. Also Austin Idol &

Dutch Mantel defeated **The Midnight Express** (Norvell Austin & Dennis Condrey) for the CWA tag team titles. Attendance was 3,841.

DragonKingKarl Note: This would be one of the last times Norvell Austin was ever part of a Midnight Express combination as just two days later the more famous duo of Dennis Condrey & Bobby Eaton with Jim Cornette as their manager was formed in Bill Watts' Mid-South wrestling company. It would be five years until Randy Rose would return to the Midnight Express with Dennis Condrey in the AWA while Bobby Eaton was partnered with Stan Lane by then. Norvell Austin and Dennis Condrey and Bobby Eaton would return to Memphis to finish up a few dates and wrap up some loose ends before the Mid-South debut show aired on television.

11-23-1983: The Bobby Eaton & Dennis Condrey version of the Midnight Express made their debut managed by Jim Cornette at the Irish McNeil's Boys Club in Shreveport, LA on Mid-South television. They defeat Rick Rood (Later known as: Rick Rude) & Mike Jackson.

Ron Bass defeated Mike Rotundo in a Bunkhouse match in Miami Beach, FL to win the Southern (FL) heavyweight title.

11-24-1983: NWA Starrcade 1983: Greensboro, NC at the Greensboro Coliseum: 15,447 attendance: Results: The Assassins (Jody Hamilton & Ray "Hercules" Hernandez) managed by Paul Jones defeated Rufus R. Jones & Bugsy McGraw… Kevin Sullivan & Mark Lewin managed by Gary Hart defeated Scott McGhee & Johnny Weaver… Abdullah the Butcher defeated Carlos Colon… Dick Slater &

Bob Orton, Jr. defeated Wahoo McDaniel & Mark Youngblood... Charlie Brown (Jimmy Valiant) defeated the Great Kabuki managed by Gary Hart to win the Mid-Atlantic TV title... Ricky Steamboat & Jay Youngblood defeated Jack & Jerry Brisco to win the NWA World tag team titles with guest referee Angelo Mosca... Roddy Piper defeated Greg Valentine in a dog collar match... Ric Flair defeated NWA World heavyweight champion Harley Race in a steel cage match to win the title. Special guest referee was Gene Kiniski.

GCW at the Omni in Atlanta, GA: Attendance: 12,000: **Thanksgiving** Tag Team Tournament: $50,000 to the winner: Jim Neidhart & King Kong Bundy defeated Tommy Rogers & Joe Lightfoot... Butch Reed & Pez Whatley defeated Randy Rose & Jimmy Randolph... The Bruise Brothers (Porkchop Cash & Troy Graham) defeated Nikolai Volkoff & Korstia Korchenko... Ronnie Garvin & Jim Duggan defeated Bob Brown & Chick Donovan... Randy Savage & Magnum TA defeated The Mongolians... Butch Reed & Pez Whatley defeated Jim Neidhart & King Kong Bundy... Bruise Brothers defeated Ronnie Garvin & Jim Duggan... Randy Savage & Magnum TA (Terry Allen) defeated Bruise Brothers... Butch Reed & Pez Whatley defeated Randy Savage & Magnum TA to win the tournament... Debbie Combs defeated Donna Day... Ted DiBiase defeated Brett Wayne Sawyer... Jake Roberts defeated Mr. Wrestling II (Johnny Walker)... Tommy Rich & Buzz Sawyer defeated The Road Warriors (Hawk & Animal).

World Class **Thanksgiving** Star Wars in Dallas, TX at Reunion Arena drawing 18,500: Johnny Mantell & Mike Reed & Jose Lothario defeated Boris Zhukov (Jim Nelson) & Black Gordman & Tonga John (Later Known As: The Barbarian)... Missing Link (Dewey Robertson) defeated Buddy Roberts... Kevin

Von Erich defeated Terry Gordy... World Class Texas champion David Von Erich defeated Kamala via DQ... Mike Von Erich defeated Skandar Akbar... World Class American tag team champions The Super Destroyers (Scott & Bill Irwin) battled Junkyard Dog & Iceman Parsons to a double DQ... Chris Adams defeated Jimmy Garvin to win the World Class American title... Kerry Von Erich defeated Michael Hayes in a loser leaves town steel cage match.

WWF: Philadelphia, PA: Spectrum: Attendance: 7,752: Televised on the PRISM Network: The Invaders (Jose Gonzalez & Johnny Rivera) defeated Iron Mike Sharpe & Mr. Fuji... Tony Garea defeated Rene Goulet... The Tonga Kid defeated Charlie Fulton... SD Jones defeated Butcher Vachon... Tito Santana defeated Big John Studd via DQ... Sgt. Slaughter fought Tony Atlas to a double DQ... Jimmy Snuka & Arnold Skaaland defeated WWF Intercontinental champion Don Muraco & Capt. Lou Albano... Rocky Johnson defeated Bob Bradley... Pat Patterson defeated Ivan Koloff... WWF champion Bob Backlund pinned the Iron Sheik.

AWA: St. Paul Civic, MN: Attendance 13,163: Little Coco & Lord Littlebrook defeat Johnny Reb & Little Tokyo... Billy Robinson defeats Bill White... Superstar Billy Graham defeats Buck Zumhofe... Brad Rheingans wrestled Mr. Saito to a Double Count Out... David Schultz wrestled Rick Martel to a Draw... The High Flyers (Greg Gagne & Jim Brunzell) defeat AWA World Tag Team champions The Sheiks (Jerry Blackwell & Ken Patera) by DQ. Special referee: Ray Stevens... AWA World Heavyweight champion Nick Bockwinkel defeats Mad Dog Vachon.

DragonKingKarl Note: Thanksgiving night in this era was huge for pro wrestling. Many territories held wrestling cards on this night. Listed here are only those who had an attendance of 5,000 or more. Just with the shows we have listed, the attendance for pro wrestling on Thanksgiving night 1983 was almost 67,000. The biggest item of note was, of course, Ric Flair regaining the National Wrestling Alliance (NWA) World heavyweight title for the second time beating Harley Race in a steel cage in Greensboro, NC. This was also the night for the famous Roddy Piper verses Greg Valentine Dog Collar Match and Ricky Steamboat & Jay Youngblood regained the NWA World tag team titles from Jack & Jerry Brisco. Butch Reed & Pez Whatley won the annual Georgia Thanksgiving Night tag team tournament. The culmination of the David Von Erich verses Kamala feud took place with David retaining the Texas title and his brother Kerry Von Erich defeated Michael Hayes in a loser leave town steel cage match. In the WWF, champion Bob Backlund gained a win over the man who would soon defeat him for the title, the Iron Sheik.

11-25-1983: In St. Louis, MO: NWA World heavyweight champion Ric Flair defeated NWA Missouri champion David Von Erich… AWA World tag team champions The Sheiks (Crusher Blackwell & Ken Patera) defeated Dick the Bruiser & Bulldog Bob Brown… Austin Idol defeated Denny Brown… Iceman Parsons defeated Blackjack Lanza… Paul Orndorff defeated Steve Olsonoski (substituting for Rick Martel)… Tiger Mask (Ken Wayne) (substituting for Buck Robley) defeated Angelo Mosca Jr… 666 (Jim Starr) defeated Ron Ritchie… Paul Kelly & Velvet McIntyre defeated Scott Farris & Peggy Lee. Attendance: 8,746

Magnum T.A. (Terry Allen) & Mr. Wrestling II (Johnny Walker) defeated Jim Neidhart & Butch Reed in a steel cage in New Orleans, LA at the Municipal Auditorium to win the Mid-South tag team titles.

11-26-1983: WWF: Landover, MD: Capital Centre: Attendance: 10,000: Bob Bradley defeated Israel Matia… Eddie Gilbert defeated Charlie Fulton… Tony Garea defeated Rene Goulet… Salvatore Bellomo fought Iron Mike Sharpe to a draw… Mr. Fuji defeated SD Jones… The Masked Superstar (Bill Eadie) defeated WWF champion Bob Backlund via count-out… Rocky Johnson defeated Big John Studd via DQ… Pat Patterson defeated Ivan Koloff via count-out… Tony Atlas fought Sgt. Slaughter to a draw… WWF Intercontinental champion Don Muraco & Capt. Lou Albano defeated Jimmy Snuka & Arnold Skaaland.

Saga of the Death of David Von Erich - World Class wrestling TV: A highlight show this week. David Von Erich is intermittently in some video clips but it mostly focuses on Kerry & Kevin Von Erich verses The Freebirds.

11-27-1983: Kevin Von Erich defeats NWA World heavyweight champion Ric Flair in a non-title match in San Antonio, TX.

11-28-1983: David Von Erich defeats NWA World heavyweight champion Ric Flair in a non-title match in Ft. Worth, TX.

Ken Lucas defeated Rip Rogers for the NWA U.S. Junior title and Robert Fuller battled Jos LeDuc to a no contest which resulted in the NWA Southeastern title being vacated in Birmingham, AL.

The Fabulous Ones (Steve Keirn & Stan Lane) defeated The Bruise Brothers (Porkchop Cash & Dream Machine) for the Southern tag team titles. Also, Terry Taylor won the Mid-America title from Buddy Landell at the Mid-South Coliseum in Memphis, TN.

11-30-1983: One Man Gang & Ron Bass defeated Dusty Rhodes & Mike Davis (substituting for Blackjack Mulligan) to win the United States tag team titles in Tampa, FL on TV.

December 1983

12-02-1983: WWF champion Bob Backlund defeated WWF Intercontinental champion Don Muraco in San Jose, CA.

12-03-1983: Dick Slater defeated Rufus R. Jones to win the Mid-Atlantic title in Hampton, VA.

Bob Armstrong won a tournament in Dothan, AL at the Houston County Farm center to win the vacant NWA Southeastern title defeating Jerry Stubbs, The Superstar (Ray Harris), Wayne Farris (Later Known As: Honky Tonk Man), and Jos LeDuc.

Saga of the Death of David Von Erich - World Class wrestling TV: Largely highlights from the Thanksgiving Star Wars show. David & Kerry & Kevin & Mike Von Erich have an interview hyping Mike's debut. Mike Von Erich verses Skandar Akbar. Sam Muchnick is sitting at ringside and is introduced. Kevin brings him out but remains away from ringside. They keep pushing Mike as the best athlete of the family when, clearly, he is not. Mike is frail, nonathletic, and uncharismatic. Skandar Akbar carries the match. Mike wins with a roll up as Akbar is trying to get his whip. Mike takes away the whip and hits Akbar. Kevin is at ringside to congratulate. David's only involvement in this episode was being in the interview.

12-04-1983: Buzz & Brett Sawyer defeated The Road Warriors for the NWA National tag team titles in the Omni in Atlanta, GA. Also on the show NWA World heavyweight champion Ric Flair defeated Tommy Rich… Buzz Sawyer battled Ted DiBiase to a double DQ… Jake Roberts defeated Pez Whatley.

Toronto, Canada: Maple Leaf Gardens: Attendance 10,003: Rudy Kay defeats Nick DeCarlo… Terry Kay wrestled Billy Red Lyons to a 15 minute draw… The Destroyer (Dick Beyer) defeats Joe Marcus… Johnny Weaver defeats Kelly Kiniski… Leo Burke defeats Keith Larson… Buddy Hart (Bret Hart) defeats The Great Kabuki… Angelo Mosca & Blackjack Mulligan defeat Sgt. Slaughter & Don Kernodle… Dog Collar And Chain Match: Roddy Piper defeats Greg Valentine.

12-05-1983: At the Mid-South Coliseum in Memphis, TN with a crowd of 8,012 Jerry Lawler defeated Randy Savage by DQ to retain the Southern title. Also on the show: The Fabulous Ones (Steve Keirn & Stan Lane) fought The Road Warriors (Hawk & Animal) to a double DQ… Angelo Poffo defeated Buddy Landell… The Grapplers (Len Denton & Tony Anthony) defeated The Jaguar (Danny Davis) & Giant Frazier (Stan Frazier)… The Moondogs (Spot & Rex) & The A Team (Don Bass & Roger Smith) & The Bruise Brothers (Porkchop Cash & Dream Machine) managed by Jimmy Hart defeated Terry Taylor & Bobby Eaton &

Stagger Lee (Koko Ware) & Robert Gibson & Art Crews & Tom Pritchard in a $5000 challenge match... Bill Dundee defeated Ricky Morton to retain the U.S. Junior title... Dutch Mantel & Austin Idol defeated The Midnight Express (Dennis Condrey & Norvell Austin) to retain the CWA tag team titles.

12-06-1983: At the WWF TV tapings in Allentown, PA: Vince K. McMahon announces that WWF champion Bob Backlund will have a mystery partner to face the Wild Samoans Afa & Sika next week on TV. This would lay the groundwork for the debut and title win of Hulk Hogan in the WWF.

12-07-1983: WWF champion Bob Backlund answers the Iron Sheik's Persian Club challenge but is attacked from behind by the Iron Sheik furthering the program between the two.

12-08-1983: New Japan Pro Wrestling: in Tokyo, Japan: Sumo Hall drawing 12,000: Shunji Kosugi beat Kazuo Yamazaki... Ryuma Go beat Masanobu Kurisu... Haruka Eigen & Nobuhiko Takada drew Kuniaki Kobayashi & Isamu Teranishi... Otto Wanz & Wayne Bridges beat Osamu Kido & Yoshiaki Fujiwara... Seiji Sakaguchi pinned Bobby Duncum... Andre the Giant & Curt Hennig beat Killer Khan & Tiger Toguchi... Tatsumi Fujinami & Kengo Kimura & Akira Maeda battled Riki Choshu & Animal Hamaguchi & Yoshiaki Yatsu to a double count out... **Hulk Hogan & Antonio Inoki** beat Adrian Adonis & Dick Murdoch to win the 4th Annual MSG Tag League tournament.

DragonKingKarl Note: Hulk Hogan is undoubtedly the hottest star in pro wrestling at the moment. In about a month he will win the WWF heavyweight championship from the Iron Sheik to kick off the lucrative and popular Hulk-A-Mania era of wrestling. In Japan, Hulk Hogan and Antonio Inoki won the prestigious MSG Tag League Tournament and he has spent most of the year as the top star in the AWA (though not champion).

12-09-1983: World Class TV taping at the Sportatorium in Dallas, TX: Ernie Ladd defeated Kamala by DQ… Chris Adams & Johnny Mantel defeated Terry Gordy & Jimmy Garvin… Kerry Von Erich & Iceman Parsons defeated Super Destroyers (Scott & Bill Irwin) by DQ… Kevin Von Erich defeated Buddy Roberts… Jimmy Garvin defeated Doug Vines… Buddy Roberts battled Johnny Mantel to a draw… Missing Link (Dewey Robertson) defeated Doug Vines.

12-10-1983: NWA World heavyweight champion Ric Flair appears on Southeastern Championship Wrestling television in Dothan, AL to further his feud with Bob Armstrong. Here he connects with his future best friend Arn Anderson who is wrestling as Super Olympia at the time. During a brawl on TV, Ric Flair, as told on his podcast, accidentally breaks his Rolex watch when he slides it too far out of the ring. This can be clearly seen on television. (Visit the When It Was Cool YouTube page to see it!)

Saga of the Death of David Von Erich - World Class wrestling TV: More Reunion arena footage this week. Video footage of David Von Erich verses Kamala and Skandar Akbar hitting David with a whip (striking the back of his head). Then an interview with David Von Erich. David is pushed as the only person to have beaten Kamala. He cuts a good tough guy promo. Then video of David Von Erich verses Kamala from Reunion Arena. Kamala is billed at 6'10" tall and

David at 6'7" tall. David is clearly a few inches taller. David is busted open during the match. Kamala literally licks his blood and starts chewing on David's forehead. David kicks out of the big splash and puts the Iron Claw on Kamala. Kamala makes the ropes. David attacks both Friday & Skandar Akbar. David wins by DQ but Kamala attacks him from behind and Akbar chokes him with his head covering. Kerry comes in for the save and bodyslams Kamala.

WWF: Boston, MA: Boston Garden: Attendance 14,750: Pete Doherty defeats Chuck Tanner… Eddie Gilbert defeats Fred Marzino… Chief Jay Strongbow defeats Iron Mike Sharpe by DQ… The Iron Sheik defeats Tony Garea… Pat Patterson defeats Ivan Koloff by Count Out… Tito Santana defeats WWF Intercontinental champion Don Muraco by Count Out… Jimmy Snuka defeats Sgt. Slaughter… WWF champion Bob Backlund defeats The Masked Superstar (Bill Eadie) … Rocky Johnson & Salvatore Bellomo defeat Charlie Fulton & Mr. Fuji.

12-11-1983: NWA World heavyweight champion Ric Flair begins a tour of Japan. In Yokosuka, Japan Giant Baba & Great Kabuki & Dory Funk, Jr. defeated Ric Flair & Barry Windham & Ron Fuller.

12-12-1983: All-Japan Pro Wrestling: in Tokyo, Japan: Sumo Hall drawing 13,000: Ashura Hara beat Goro Tsurumi… Mighty Inoue beat The Mongolian… Mil Mascaras & Dos Caras beat Barry Windham & Ron Fuller… Giant Baba & Dory Funk, Jr. beat Professor Ito & Tiger Jeet Singh… NWA World champion Ric Flair beat Great Kabuki via DQ… Stan Hansen & Bruiser Brody beat Jumbo Tsuruta & Genichiro Tenryu to win the 1983 Real World Tag League tournament.

At the Mid-South Coliseum in Memphis, TN in a steel cage match Jerry Lawler defeated Randy Savage by DQ to retain the Southern title. Attendance was 4,500.

12-13-1983: Dick Slater defeated NWA U.S. champion Greg Valentine to win the title in Shelby, NC.

12-16-1983: Mike Rotundo defeated Greg Valentine to win the vacant Florida title in St. Petersburg, FL.

WWF: Pittsburgh, PA: Civic Arena: Attendance: 5,992: SD Jones pinned the Beast... The Iron Sheik pinned Salvatore Bellomo... WWF Intercontinental champion Don Muraco & Capt. Lou Albano defeated Jimmy Snuka & Arnold Skaaland... The Masked Superstar (Bill Eadie) defeated WWF champion Bob Backlund via count-out... Sgt. Slaughter defeated Ivan Putski via count-out... Eddie Gilbert pinned Bill Dixon... Tony Atlas pinned Mr. Fuji.

12-17-1983: Saga of the Death of David Von Erich - World Class wrestling TV: No mention of David Von Erich on this episode as it focused on the feud between The Super Destroyers (Scott & Bill Irwin) with their manager Skandar Akbar and Kerry Von Erich & Iceman Parsons.

12-18-1983: Carlos Colon defeated NWA World heavyweight champion Ric Flair in a no DQ steel cage match in Bayamon, Puerto Rico but did not win the title.

Barry Windham begins wrestling under a mask in Florida as the Dirty Yellow Dog.

12-24-1983: Kevin Von Erich defeated NWA World heavyweight champion Ric Flair in San Antonio, TX but did not win the title.

Saga of the Death of David Von Erich - World Class wrestling TV: David Von Erich music video is played.

12-25-1983: World Class Championship Wrestling (WCCW) Star Wars: Dallas, TX: Reunion Arena: 19,675 attendance. Results: Missing Link (Dewey Robertson) defeated Johnny Mantell... Iceman King Parsons & Brian Adias defeated the American tag team champions the Super Destroyers (Scott & Bill Irwin) to win the titles... Kerry Von Erich defeated Kamala by DQ... Mike Reed defeated The Mongol (Gene Petit)... David Von Erich defeated NWA World heavyweight champion Ric Flair via DQ... Jose Lothario defeated Black Gordman... Jimmy Garvin defeated American champion Chris Adams to win the title... Kevin & Mike Von Erich defeated Terry Gordy & Buddy Roberts in a no DQ loser leaves town match for one year.

American Wrestling Association (AWA) Christmas Day Show: St. Paul, MN: 18,000 attendance: Mad Dog Vachon defeated AWA World heavyweight champion Nick Bockwinkel by DQ... The Highfliers (Greg Gagne & Jim Brunzell) & Baron Von Raschke & Ray Stevens defeated The Sheiks (Ken Patera & Jerry Blackwell) & Mr. Saito & Sheik Adnan Al Kassie... Jesse Ventura defeated Steve Olsonoski... Rick Martel defeated Superstar Billy Graham by DQ... Billy Robinson wrestled Brad Rheingans to a draw... Buck Zumhofe defeated Bill White.

GCW at the Omni in Atlanta, GA: Ted DiBiase defeated Tommy Rich... Buzz Sawyer defeated The Sheik... Stan Hansen & Bugsy McGraw defeated The Road Warriors (Hawk & Animal) by DQ... Lights Out Match: Buzz Sawyer defeated Paul Ellering... Brett Wayne Sawyer defeated Jake Roberts... Les Thornton defeated Tommy Rogers.

12-26-1983: In Memphis, TN: Mid-South Coliseum drawing 6,450: Angelo Poffo beat Jim Jamieson... Plowboy Frazier (Stan Frazier) beat Robert Reed & Ken Raper in a handicap match... Stagger Lee (Koko Ware) & Dutch Mantel beat The Moondogs (Rex & Spot)... Penny Mitchell & Darling Dagmar beat Donna Christanello & Diamond Lil... Norvell Austin & Sabu (Coco Samoa) beat Art Crews & The Jaguar (Danny Davis)... The Grapplers (Len Denton & Tony Anthony) beat Porkchop Cash & Dream Machine (Troy Graham) in a losers no longer managed by Jimmy Hart match... The Rock-n-Roll Express (Ricky Morton & Robert Gibson) beat The A-Team (Don Bass & Roger Smith) via DQ... Randy Savage beat Terry Taylor to win the Mid-America title... Steve Keirn pinned Bill Dundee in a loser leaves town match... Jerry Lawler beat Austin Idol.

Bruiser Brody defeated NWA World heavyweight champion Ric Flair by DQ in Toronto, Canada.

Rip Rogers defeated Ken Lucas to win the NWA U.S. Junior title in Birmingham, AL. Also on the show Jerry Stubbs defeated Bob Armstrong for the NWA Southeastern title.

WWF in New York City, NY at Madison Square Garden in front of 26,592 fans. Results: Jose Luis Rivera defeated Rene Goulet... Salvatore Bellomo battled Tiger Chung Lee to a draw... Jimmy Snuka & Arnold Skaaland defeated Don Muraco & Captain Lou Albano... Sgt. Slaughter defeated Chief Jay Strongbow... Masked Superstar (Bill Eadie) battled Ivan Putski to a double DQ... **Iron Sheik, managed by Freddie Blassie defeated WWF champion Bob Backlund to win the WWF title when manager Arnold Skaaland threw in the towel**... Wild Samoans (Afa & Sika & Samula) defeated SD Jones & Rocky Johnson & Tony Atlas in a best 2 out of 3 falls match... Tito Santana defeated Ivan Koloff... The Invaders (Jose Gonzalez & Johnny Rivera) defeated Iron Mike Sharpe & Butcher Vachon.

DragonKingKarl Note: A very famous moment in pro wrestling history setting up the coming of Hulk-A-Mania. The Iron Sheik (Hossein Khosrow Ali Viziri) ends the WWF title reign of Bob Backlund which has lasted since February 20, 1978 (aside from an unrecognized disputed swap with Antonio Inoki in 1979) lasting a total of 2,135 days.

12-27-1983: WWF champion the Iron Sheik makes his first title defense in Lancaster, PA defeating Chief Jay Strongbow.

In St. Louis, MO WWF holds another show at the Chase Park Hotel with a crowd of 1100 fans where Hulk Hogan makes his WWF return defeating Bill Dixon.

12-29-1983: WWF champion Iron Sheik defeated Salvatore Bellomo in Landover, MD in a title defense.

12-30-1983: WWF champion Iron Sheik defeats Pat Patterson by DQ to retain the title in Salisbury, MD.

In Houston, TX: AWA World champion Nick Bockwinkel defeated Mr. Wrestling II (Johnny Walker) by DQ.

12-31-1983: **Saga of the Death of David Von Erich** - World Class wrestling TV: Highlights from the Christmas Star Wars card. Kerry Von Erich defeats Kamala by DQ. Kerry Von Erich bodyslams Kamala again. Kevin Von Erich comes in for backup. David Von Erich does not appear on the show.

The When It Was Cool Article on Major 1983 Wrestling Personality Sgt. Slaughter by Karl Stern

Sgt. Slaughter in the Wrestling Observer Hall of Fame: The Case is Complicated.

By: Karl Stern

I have been thinking a lot about Sgt. Slaughter lately. Sgt. Slaughter was all over my childhood experience. I was a big pro wrestling fan from the late 1970s into the 1980s when Sgt. Slaughter was a very popular pro wrestling star. I was also a huge comic book reader and action figure collector and became a fan of the G.I. Joe comic book series by Marvel Comics and the Hasbro action figure line. Sgt. Slaughter would become a major part of that franchise also.

Sgt. Slaughter played a great stereotypical Marine Drill Sergeant in the style of R. Lee Ermy's Gunnery Sergeant Hartman in the 1987 film Full Metal Jacket… only Sgt. Slaughter did it first. In the pages of the Weston family of pro wrestling magazines (often referred to as the Apter Magazines by wrestling fans after editor Bill Apter) I cheered Sgt. Slaughter as he battled America's enemy the Iron Sheik and had classic matches with Pat Patterson in the WWF (now WWE).

Later on, by way of videotape, I would learn of his classic matches and interviews as a heel (pro wrestling vernacular for the bad guy) for Jim Crockett Promotions and the WWF. In 1985 Sgt. Slaughter would leave the WWF following a merchandising dispute and would license his character to the Hasbro G.I. Joe franchise which would produce multiple action figures based on Sgt. Slaughter. He would also appear briefly in the Marvel Comic books *G.I. Joe: A Real American Hero* comic series and extensively on the G.I. Joe cartoons and the G.I. Joe animated movie. It was a great time to be a Sgt. Slaughter fan.

His wrestling career, however, stuttered a little after that point. He began being more associated with G.I. Joe and action figures than with pro wrestling, despite the fact he was a top star in the Minnesota based AWA wrestling promotion. His work declined. He put on a little too much weight. He seemed to get, and I hate to use this word because I truly love Sgt. Slaughter, lazy. In 1999, *Wrestling Observer Newsletter* editor Dave Meltzer had this to say about Sgt. Slaughter's qualifications to be in the *Wrestling Observer Newsletter Hall of Fame*, "Slaughter in the early 1980s Carolina's and WWF was one of the best working big-men of his time and a very effective heel. In 1984, Slaughter for a short period of time was probably behind only Hulk Hogan as the top babyface in the entire business, but his work fell off from there and he spent years living off his one big year in the WWF. I don't see him as a Hall of Famer."

And that is why I've been thinking a lot about Sgt. Slaughter lately. I am a voter for the *Wrestling Observer Hall of Fame* and, for over a decade, I have dutifully filled out my ballot every year and sent it in. I would like to think my research and trumpeting might have had something to do with pioneer Col. James H. McLaughlin getting in a few years ago. I take my vote very seriously. Slaughter, by the way, in 2019 got 51% of the vote falling just short of the needed 60% to be inducted.

However, Dave Meltzer and I differ on Sgt. Slaughter. In my mind, I see him as a pro wrestling Hall of Famer with no qualms about it. Dave feels a little differently. By 2017 Dave Meltzer had softened his stance slightly but was still anti-Slaughter, again citing his short time as a major top tier wrestler, "Sgt. Slaughter had a 1979-1984 run where he was a Hall of Fame level performer. He was a big guy who was a great worker, involved in some amazing feuds (Pat Patterson, Iron Sheik, Ricky Steamboat & Jay Youngblood, Wahoo McDaniel) and drew. It's like the others who had a big successful run. Is it enough? That's a question. If there are those who had twenty year runs in a top position, then three to six years isn't as impressive. Sgt. Slaughter was also very famous, due to time, place and gimmick, being the prototype for G.I. Joe."

Sgt. Slaughter was not, by the way, the prototype for G.I. Joe, but I concede the point and won't squabble over semantics. He was a great fit for the well established brand and gave them an honest to goodness real life spokesperson for the toy line which I loved very dearly.

I respectfully disagree with Dave's belief that Sgt. Slaughter wasn't a big time star long enough. While I would have liked to have seen his era of super-stardom run a little longer myself, his cultural impact more than makes up for the abbreviated five year window where his work was top notch. It also should be noted that his biggest accolade in the pro wrestling business came outside of that five year window when, on January 19, 1991, he won the WWF heavyweight title from the Ultimate Warrior in Miami, FL to hold the most pop culturally relevant championship in professional wrestling.

That starring role as WWF heavyweight champion did not come without controversy. As noted, Sgt. Slaughter's best days in the ring were behind him by that point and he had been repackaged as a traitor. A turncoat heel who was no longer a brutal, but patriotic, Marine Corps Drill Instructor, instead he was an Iraqi sympathizer who touted the praises of Saddam Hussein while the first Gulf War raged. Even by WWE's often questionable standards, this storyline was tasteless.

The story, simplistic as it was, set in motion events that would return the former top babyface in pro wrestling, Hulk Hogan, to become the WWF heavyweight champion again. America would, in fact, win out. Sgt. Slaughter would later, in the storyline, repent for his sins and try to get his country back. All of this was ill advised and none of it worked out very well.

It was underwhelming to the degree that, WWF WrestleMania 7, originally slated for the Los Angeles Coliseum, was moved to the much smaller Los Angeles Sports Arena cutting the anticipated attendance of 100,000 people down to the actual attendance of 16,158. WWF (WWE) told the press that the move was for security reasons due to the heat generated from the turncoat angle and the Gulf War creating security concerns. Many wrestling insider's and newsletters insist that it was actually due to poor ticket sales.

No matter the actual reason, the storyline was tasteless and essentially signaled the end to Sgt. Slaughter as a main event level drawing card. Sgt. Slaughter's deal with Hasbro had also long ended but Slaughter would remain around the WWF (WWE) for years to come in various roles both behind the scenes and in front of the camera. Everybody, it seemed, liked Sgt. Slaughter.

However, Sgt. Slaughter is the name of a character. The man behind the character is actually Robert Rudolph Remus, born August 27, 1948, and here is where things get complicated.

You see, pro wrestling, as silly as it seems, used to adhere to a bizarre code of conduct called "Kayfabe". It's an old carnival (or carny) term which essentially means "to keep up appearances" or act like this insanity is real. Yes, despite the fact that newspapers routinely called pro wrestling "fake" in the 1800's, and despite the fact that actors have been respected for acting since antiquity (could you imagine a Shakespearean actor having to keep up the pretense that they were actually a Denmark Prince named Hamlet?) pro wrestling somehow felt the need to act real.

Make no mistake, it was a fun act to a degree. Also, pro wrestling was never fake. While wrestling finishes were predetermined and the participants were working with one another to entertain the crowd, pro wrestling involved tremendous athleticism and showmanship. Pro wrestling is no more fake than a circus trapeze artist. There is also no shame in being what you are.

John Rambo was an interesting character created and portrayed by Sylvester Stallone. A character he played in several movies. Yet, no one expects Stallone to pretend he was actually a Vietnam veteran with an ax to grind against society. Does anyone actually think Harrison Ford splits his time between searching for the Ark of the Covenant and traveling a distant galaxy with a giant space ape? Of course not. But for some reason the actor-athletes who are professional wrestlers, especially from Sgt. Slaughter's era, feel compelled to "keep up the act".

And that is where Sgt. Slaughter and I part company and why, this past year I could not, in good conscience, vote for him in the *Wrestling Observer Newsletter Hall of Fame*.

In recent years, wrestling has come out of the proverbial closet. It's no longer a secret what it really is and that is fine. Wrestling is a show. Just as *Game of Thrones* was a show, just as *Star Wars* is a show, just as *Joker* was a show. It is very skillful actor-athletes putting on a performance. And that's OK. In fact, done well, it can be exceptionally entertaining. A new type of interview has emerged over the last decade called the "shoot interview". That phrase may sound strange to the uninitiated but a "shoot" in pro wrestling lingo means "real or legitimate". It's the difference between talking to Rambo and talking to Sylvester Stallone.

Yet, time and time again, in these "shoot" segments or interviews, or in a context where Bob Remus is talking and not Sgt. Slaughter (such as a newspaper interview), Robert Remus has sometimes outright stated or been coy about his actual military service.

Wait, Sgt. Slaughter was actually a member of the United States Marine Corps right? Well, yes. I suppose, in fiction, the character of Sgt. Slaughter was a Drill Sergeant in the United States Marine Corps just as much as he was part of the anti-terrorist organization G.I. Joe out to stop the forces of Cobra. Robert Remus, however, maybe not so much.

To say that Robert Remus has been vague, or at least misleading, about his actual service in the U.S. military is putting it mildly. His Wikipedia page, which can be edited by anyone including, presumably Robert Remus, states clearly that, "Remus legitimately enlisted in the United States Marine Corps…" (As of January 8, 2020 anyway)

You will notice a citation about that fact as footnote "5" which directs to an unsourced article called "Cereal Liars'' which states without any citation of its own that "Sgt. Slaughter comes about his military rank legitimately…"

UPDATE: Following publication of this article at WhenItWasCool.com the Wikipedia page has been updated to state he was not in the Marine Corps citing the *Baltimore Sun* article from 1985.

Not so fast says the *Baltimore Sun* newspaper in a March 24, 1985 article. The article states, "Government records reveal Slaughter, a.k.a. Robert Remus, never served time in the U.S. Marine Corps, though he claims to have been a drill instructor from 1966 to 1973." According to the article, the USMC even sent a letter to Robert Remus telling him to stop representing himself as a former Marine.

That isn't what happened however. In the thirty-five years since then, Robert Remus has continued to either state he was in the Marine Corps or side step the question. An interview posted on YouTube has Remus saying he did two tours of duty in Vietnam. Another print interview quotes him as saying, "I was actually born in Beaufort, S.C. My father was in the Marine Corps at Parris Island and we lived on a farm back in Minnesota. When he was out of the Corps we moved back there. When it was time for me to get out of high school, [my parents] really couldn't afford to send me to college, so my father suggested maybe I want to join the Corps, join the military service and maybe do college later. So I thought, "Well, that's probably what I'll do, so I'll go into the Marine Corps and I'll go to college when I get out." I got halfway there, ended up at a pro wrestling training camp on leave, and I got into a little scuffle with the British Empire champion Billy Robertson and I knew that's what I wanted to do." In the same sentence he seems to say he backed out of going to the Marines "halfway there" yet went to wrestling camp while "on leave".

As recently as July 2019 in an article from the *Miami Herald*, Remus is mixing reality with the fantasy of being a real Marine drill instructor.

Sgt. Slaughter, the character, can say anything he wants. He's fictional, so I guess he can have any sort of backstory he, Hasbro, or WWE pleases. I'm not even throwing an outrage over stolen valor or anything that sinister. But I do think there needs to be a line of respect drawn. The United States military and the United States Marine Corps are full of people who sacrifice and serve their country. Some even die for it. Post Traumatic Stress Disorder (PTSD) and depression is leading to, on average, 22 people per day taking their lives because of real, not fake, military service and the hardships, stress, and trauma that comes with it.

I cannot in good conscience vote for the character of Sgt. Slaughter to be included in the *Wrestling Observer Hall of Fame* until the human being Robert Remus stops doing this. I am not even going so far as to ask for an apology or retraction, though I would gladly print it if one came. And absolutely, without question or hesitation, if Robert Remus provided some sort of evidence or proof he ever signed up for the United States Marine Corps and what his actual real status was I would certainly include that here and give the man the credit he is due.

I love G.I. Joe. I love pro wrestling. I love the character of Sgt. Slaughter. I humbly ask the man who is Robert Remus to consider setting the record straight. There is no shame in being a great character, I would argue a Hall of Fame character. No shame at all in a job well done. Just be clear and don't steal nor diminish the valor of true real American heroes while doing so.

Assorted Notes and Facts From 1983

The 1983 *Pro Wrestling Illustrated* magazine wrestler of the Year: Harley Race

The 1983 *Pro Wrestling Illustrated* magazine tag team of the Year: The Road Warriors (Hawk & Animal)

The 1983 *Pro Wrestling Illustrated* magazine Match of the Year: Starrcade: Ric Flair defeats Harley Race for the NWA World title in a Steel Cage

The 1983 *Pro Wrestling Illustrated* magazine Most Popular Wrestler of the Year: Jimmy "Superfly" Snuka

The 1983 *Pro Wrestling Illustrated* magazine Most Hated Wrestler of the Year: Greg "The Hammer" Valentine

The 1983 *Pro Wrestling Illustrated* magazine Most Improved Wrestler of the Year: Brett Wayne Sawyer

The 1983 *Pro Wrestling Illustrated* magazine Inspirational Wrestler of the Year: Hulk Hogan

The 1983 *Pro Wrestling Illustrated* magazine Rookie of the Year: Angelo Mosca, Jr.

The 1983 *Pro Wrestling Illustrated* magazine Manager of the Year: James J. Dillon

The 1983 *Pro Wrestling Illustrated* magazine Editor's Award: The Grand Wizard

The 1983 *Wrestling Observer Newsletter* Wrestler of the Year: Ric Flair

The 1983 *Wrestling Observer Newsletter* Feud of the Year: The Freebirds verses The Von Erichs

The 1983 *Wrestling Observer Newsletter* Tag Team of the Year: Ricky Steamboat & Jay Youngblood

The 1983 *Wrestling Observer Newsletter* Most Improved Wrestler of the Year: Curt Hennig

The 1983 *Wrestling Observer Newsletter* Best on Interviews: Roddy Piper

Major Wrestling Personalities Who Were Born in 1983:

Chris Masters

Maryse Ouellet

Davey Richards

Timothy Thatcher

Ethan Carter III (AKA: EC3)

Evan Bourne

Scorpio Sky

Bushi

Tanga Loa

"Filthy" Tom Lawlor

Leva Bates

Alex Shelley

Brandi Rhodes

Heath Slater

Roderick Strong

Braun Strowman

Kenny Omega

Taya Valkyrie

Nikki Bella

Brie Bella

Rene Dupree

Luke Gallows

Eddie Edwards

Major Wrestling Personalities Who Died in 1983:

Mayes McLain

Frank Tunney

Johnny Rougeau

Jack Dempsey (Legendary boxer who also refereed a considerable number of pro wrestling matches.)

The Grand Wizard

Earl McCready

Finally, the 1983 When It Was Cool Guide to Pop Culture

WhenItWasCool.com not only covers pro wrestling history (though that is probably what we are best known for presently) but we also cover retro pop culture. To fully understand professional wrestling in context, it is also important to know what was going on in popular culture. Movies, music, TV, and other sports impact and influence pro wrestling characters and angles tremendously. During 1983, Hulk Hogan used the theme song to *Rocky III: Eye of the Tiger* because he was associated with that movie. The menace of The Road Warriors was greatly enhanced by their use of the Black Sabbath song *Iron Man*. Terry Allen's Magnum T.A. name was a direct rip-off from the TV show Magnum P.I. due to Terry Allen's resemblance to actor Tom Sellak, and so on it goes.

So, to help contextualize the world in which 1983 pro wrestling existed, here is our feature article from WhenItWasCool.com: *A Guide to 1983 Pop Culture*.

1983 - Your complete When It Was Cool Guide to the year 1983 in pop-culture, music, and more.

By: Karl Stern

I turned twelve years old in 1983 so obviously it has a special place in my heart. This is part of an on-going series of extensive "Year in Review" guides to the greatest years of When It Was Cool retro pop-culture. But please remember, we need your help to keep our website going so consider helping us out on Patreon.

Check out our free podcast bonus show looking back at 1983 and be sure to subscribe to the When It Was Cool Podcast!

10 Major Events that Happened in 1983:

01-30-1983: The Washington Redskins won their first NFL Super Bowl defeating the Miami Dolphins following a short season due to a players strike. Super Bowl XVII saw the AFC champion Miami Dolphins and the NFC champion Washington Redskins face off following the short 1982 NFL season with only 9 regular games due to the strike. The Redskins defeated the Dolphins by the score of 27–17 to win their first ever Super Bowl championship. The game was played on January 30, 1983 at the Rose Bowl in Pasadena, California.

02-20-1983: Cale Yarborough won the 25th Daytona 500 NASCAR race in Daytona Beach, Florida.

02-28-1983: The final episode of *M.A.S.H.* airs drawing 105.97 million total viewers and a total audience of 121.6 million which was more than both Super Bowl XVII and the successful *Roots* miniseries. The episode surpassed the single-episode ratings record that had been set by the *Dallas* episode that resolved the "*Who Shot J.R.?*" cliffhanger.

03-25-1983: Motown celebrates its 25th anniversary with a television special *Motown 25: Yesterday*, Today, Forever, during which Michael Jackson performs "*Billie Jean*" and introduces the moonwalk. (A dance move frequently used by Freebirds member Michael Hayes).

05-25-1983: *Star Wars: Return of the Jedi* is released in theaters marking the last movie of the original Star Wars trilogy. The movie trilogy's main antagonist, Darth Vader, finds redemption in the end.

09-01-1983: Korean Air Lines Flight 007 is shot down by a Soviet Union Air Force fighter near Moneron Island when the commercial aircraft enters Soviet airspace. All 269 on board were killed, including U.S. Congressman Larry McDonald, causing a significant escalation in the Cold War between the United States and the Soviet Union. (Austin Idol would reference this in an interview verses opponent Boris Zhukov)

09-18-1983: The rock band KISS appeared for the first time in public without their makeup on MTV.

10-16-1983: Baltimore Orioles beat the Philadelphia Phillies 4 games to 1 to win the World series. This was the first World Series since 1956 in which the teams did not use air travel. Baltimore and Philadelphia are approximately 100 miles apart.

10-23-1983: Beirut barracks bombing: Simultaneous suicide truck-bombings destroy both the French Army and United States Marine Corps barracks in Beirut, killing 241 U.S. servicemen, 58 French paratroopers and 6 Lebanese civilians.

10-25-1983: The Invasion of Grenada was a 1983 United States led invasion of the Caribbean island nation of Grenada, which has a population of about 91,000 that resulted in a U.S. victory within a matter of weeks. Codenamed: Operation Urgent Fury, it was triggered by the internal strife within the People's Revolutionary Government that resulted in the house arrest and the execution of the previous leader and second Prime minister of Grenada Maurice Bishop. The invasion resulted in the appointment of an interim government, followed by democratic elections in 1984. The country has remained a democratic nation since then.

The Billboard Top 100 Songs of 1983

1. "Every Breath You Take"- The Police

2. "Billie Jean"- Michael Jackson

3. "Flashdance... What a Feeling"- Irene Cara

4. "Down Under"- Men at Work

5. "Beat It"- Michael Jackson

6. "Total Eclipse of the Heart"- Bonnie Tyler

7. "Maneater"- Hall & Oates

8. "Baby, Come to Me"- Patti Austin and James Ingram

9. "Maniac"- Michael Sembello

10. "Sweet Dreams (Are Made of This)"- Eurythmics

11. "Do You Really Want to Hurt Me"- Culture Club

12. "You and I"- Eddie Rabbitt and Crystal Gayle

13. "Come On Eileen"- Dexys Midnight Runners

14. "Shame on the Moon"- Bob Seger & The Silver Bullet Band

15. "She Works Hard for the Money"- Donna Summer

16. "Never Gonna Let You Go"- Sérgio Mendes

17. "Hungry Like the Wolf"- Duran Duran

18. "Let's Dance"- David Bowie

19. "Twilight Zone"- Golden Earring

20. "I Know There's Something Going On"- Frida

21. "Jeopardy"- The Greg Kihn Band

22. "Electric Avenue"- Eddy Grant

23. "She Blinded Me with Science"- Thomas Dolby

24. "Africa"- Toto

25. "Little Red Corvette"- Prince

26. "Back on the Chain Gang"- The Pretenders

27. "Up Where We Belong"- Joe Cocker and Jennifer Warnes

28. "Mr. Roboto"- Styx

29. "You Are"- Lionel Richie

30. "Der Kommissar"- After the Fire

31. "Puttin' on the Ritz"- Taco

32. "Sexual Healing"- Marvin Gaye

33. "(Keep Feeling) Fascination"- The Human League

34. "Time (Clock of the Heart)"- Culture Club

35. "The Safety Dance"- Men Without Hats

36. "Mickey"- Toni Basil

37. "You Can't Hurry Love"- Phil Collins

38. "Separate Ways (Worlds Apart)"- Journey

39. "One on One"- Hall & Oates

40. "We've Got Tonight"- Kenny Rogers & Sheena Easton

41. "1999"- Prince

42. "Stray Cat Strut"- Stray Cats

43. "Allentown"- Billy Joel

44. "Stand Back"- Stevie Nicks

45. "Tell Her About It"- Billy Joel

46. "Always Something There to Remind Me"- Naked Eyes

47. "Truly"- Lionel Richie

48. "Dirty Laundry"- Don Henley

49. "The Girl Is Mine"- Michael Jackson and Paul McCartney

50. "Too Shy"- Kajagoogoo

51. "Goody Two-Shoes"- Adam Ant

52. "Rock the Casbah"- The Clash

53. "Our House"- Madness

54. "Overkill"- Men at Work

55. "Is There Something I Should Know?"- Duran Duran

56. "Gloria"- Laura Branigan

57. "Affair of the Heart"- Rick Springfield

58. "She's a Beauty"- The Tubes

59. "Solitaire"- Laura Branigan

60. "Don't Let It End"- Styx

61. "How Am I Supposed to Live Without You"- Laura Branigan

62. "China Girl"- David Bowie

63. "Come Dancing"- The Kinks

64. "Promises, Promises"- Naked Eyes

65. "The Other Guy"- Little River Band

66. "Making Love Out of Nothing at All"- Air Supply

67. "Family Man"- Hall & Oates

68. "Wanna Be Startin' Somethin'"- Michael Jackson

69. "I Won't Hold You Back"- Toto

70. "All Right"- Christopher Cross

71. "Straight from the Heart"- Bryan Adams

72. "Heart to Heart"- Kenny Loggins

73. "My Love"- Lionel Richie

74. "I'm Still Standing"- Elton John

75. "Hot Girls in Love"- Loverboy

76. "It's a Mistake"- Men at Work

77. "I'll Tumble 4 Ya"- Culture Club

78. "All This Love"- DeBarge

79. "Your Love Is Driving Me Crazy"- Sammy Hagar

80. "Heartbreaker"- Dionne Warwick

81. "Faithfully"- Journey

82. "Steppin' Out"- Joe Jackson

83. "Take Me to Heart"- Quarterflash

84. "(She's) Sexy + 17"- Stray Cats

85. "Try Again"- Champaign

86. "Dead Giveaway"- Shalamar

87. "Lawyers in Love"- Jackson Browne

88. "What About Me"- Moving Pictures

89. "Human Nature"- Michael Jackson

90. "Photograph"- Def Leppard

91. "Pass the Dutchie"- Musical Youth

92. "True"- Spandau Ballet

93. "Far from Over"- Frank Stallone

94. "I've Got a Rock 'n' Roll Heart"- Eric Clapton

95. "It Might Be You"- Stephen Bishop

96. "Tonight, I Celebrate My Love"- Peabo Bryson and Roberta Flack

97. "You Got Lucky"- Tom Petty and the Heartbreakers

98. "Don't Cry"- Asia

99. "Breaking Us in Two"- Joe Jackson

100. "Fall in Love with Me"- Earth, Wind & Fire

The great country music legend Don Williams scored two number one hit country music songs in 1983: *Love is on a Roll* and *If Hollywood Don't Need You*.

Metallica's *Kill 'Em All* is released. The When It Was Cool resident thrash heavy metal expert NoFriender of the *NoFriender Thrash Metal Show* had this to say about the album, "Metallica's Kill Em All was released on 07-25-1983, which is the BC/AD dividing line for the genre of thrash metal."

G.I. Joe Swivel Arm Battle Grip feature introduced: The original 1982 wave of G.I. Joe action figures were reintroduced but this time with arms that swiveled allowing them to hold their accessories and weapons better. This was a major innovation in action figure articulation. A second wave of G.I. Joe action figures were also released including Gung-Ho, Major Bludd, Destro, and more.

Atari 5200 Gaming System released: The Atari 5200 Super-system was introduced in 1982 and became the primary home video game system in homes during 1983. It was a higher-end complementary console for the popular Atari 2600. The 5200 was created to compete with the Intellivision, but wound up more directly competing with the ColecoVision shortly after its release.

Cabbage Patch Kids became a sensation: Cabbage Patch Kids were created by Xavier Roberts and registered in the United States copyright office in 1978. Originally Roberts called these hand-stitched, one-of-a-kind, soft fabric sculptures "The Little People". His Little People were not offered for sale, but were "adopted" each with their own individual name and birth certificate and often referred to as "Adoption Dolls". The doll brand went on to become one of the most popular toy fads of the 1980s and one of the longest-running doll franchises in America. The name change to Cabbage Patch Kids was made in 1982 when Xavier's company, Original Appalachian Artworks, began to license a smaller version of the handmade creations to a toy manufacturer named Coleco.

Hasbro Glo Worm: Glo Worm is a stuffed toy by Hasbro's Playskool division. Introduced in 1982, the plush body contained a battery-powered device that when squeezed would light up the toy's vinyl head from within, creating a soft glow. The toy, upon release, was such a success that Hasbro released a series of story books, night lights, videos and other merchandise that continued until the early 1990s.

Top 25 Movies of 1983:

1. Scarface: In Miami in 1980, a determined Cuban immigrant takes over a drug cartel and succumbs to greed. Director: Brian De Palma - Stars: Al Pacino, Michelle Pfeiffer, Steven Bauer, Mary Elizabeth Mastrantonio. Gross: $44.70M

2. Trading Places: A snobbish investor and a wily street con artist find their positions reversed as part of a bet by two callous millionaires. Director: John Landis - Stars: Eddie Murphy, Dan Aykroyd, Ralph Bellamy, Don Ameche. Gross: $90.40M

3. The Outsiders: The rivalry between two gangs, the poor Greasers and the rich Socs, only heats up when one gang member kills a member of the other. Director: Francis Ford Coppola - Stars: C. Thomas Howell, Matt Dillon, Ralph Macchio, Patrick Swayze. Gross: $25.60M

4. Star Wars: Episode VI - Return of the Jedi: After a daring mission to rescue Han Solo from Jabba the Hutt, the rebels dispatch to Endor to destroy a more powerful Death Star. Meanwhile, Luke struggles to help Vader back from the dark side without falling into the Emperor's trap. Director: Richard Marquand - Stars: Mark Hamill, Harrison Ford, Carrie Fisher, Billy Dee Williams. Gross: $309.13M

5. Jaws 3-D: The sons of police chief Brody must protect civilians at a SeaWorld theme park after a 35-foot shark becomes trapped in the park with them. Director: Joe Alves - Stars: Dennis Quaid, Bess Armstrong, Simon MacCorkindale, Louis Gossett Jr. Gross: $42.20M

6. Christine: A nerdish boy buys a strange car with an evil mind of its own and his nature starts to change to reflect it. Director: John Carpenter - Stars: Keith Gordon, John Stockwell, Alexandra Paul, Robert Prosky. Gross: $21.20M

7. National Lampoon's Vacation: The Griswold family's cross-country drive to the Walley World theme park proves to be much more arduous than they ever anticipated. Director: Harold Ramis - Stars: Chevy Chase, Beverly D'Angelo, Imogene Coca, Randy Quaid. Gross: $61.40M

8. Risky Business: A Chicago teenager is looking for fun at home while his parents are away, but the situation quickly gets out of hand. Director: Paul Brickman - Stars: Tom Cruise, Rebecca De Mornay, Joe Pantoliano, Richard Masur. Gross: $63.50M

9. Cujo: Cujo, a friendly St. Bernard, contracts rabies and conducts a reign of terror on a small American town. Director: Lewis Teague - Stars: Dee Wallace, Daniel Hugh Kelly, Danny Pintauro, Christopher Stone. Gross: $21.20M

10. The Dead Zone: A man awakens from a coma to discover he has a psychic ability. Director: David Cronenberg - Stars: Christopher Walken, Brooke Adams, Tom Skerritt, Herbert Lom

11. Flashdance: A Pittsburgh woman with two jobs as a welder and an exotic dancer wants to get into ballet school. Director: Adrian Lyne - Stars: Jennifer Beals, Michael Nouri, Lilia Skala, Sunny Johnson. Gross: $94.90M

12. WarGames: "Shall we play a game?" A young man finds a back door into a military central computer in which reality is confused with game-playing, possibly starting World War III. Director: John Badham - Stars: Matthew Broderick, Ally Sheedy, John Wood, Dabney Coleman. Gross: $79.57M

13. Mr. Mom: After he's laid off, a husband switches roles with his wife. She returns to the workforce, and he becomes a stay-at-home dad, a job he has no clue how to do. Director: Stan Dragoti - Stars: Michael Keaton, Teri Garr, Frederick Koehler, Taliesin Jaffe. Gross: $64.80M

14. All the Right Moves: A high school football player desperate for a scholarship and his headstrong coach clash in a dying Pennsylvania steel town. Director: Michael Chapman - Stars: Tom Cruise, Lea Thompson, Craig T. Nelson, Charles Cioffi

15. Octopussy: A fake Fabergé egg and a fellow agent's death lead James Bond to uncover an international jewel-smuggling operation, headed by the mysterious Octopussy, being used to disguise a nuclear attack on N.A.T.O. forces. Director: John Glen - Stars: Roger Moore, Maud Adams, Louis Jourdan, Kristina Wayborn. Gross: $67.90M

16. Staying Alive: It's five years later and Tony Manero's Saturday Night Fever is still burning. Now he's strutting toward his biggest challenge yet - succeeding as a dancer on the Broadway stage. Director: Sylvester Stallone - Stars: John Travolta, Cynthia Rhodes, Finola Hughes, Steve Inwood. Gross: $63.80M

17. Terms of Endearment: Follows hard-to-please Aurora looking for love and her daughter's family problems. Director: James L. Brooks - Stars: Shirley MacLaine, Debra Winger, Jack Nicholson, Danny DeVito. Gross: $108.42M

18. Never Say Never Again: A SPECTRE agent has stolen two American nuclear warheads, and James Bond must find their targets before they are detonated. Director: Irvin Kershner - Stars: Sean Connery, Kim Basinger, Klaus Maria Brandauer, Max von Sydow. Gross: $55.50M

19. Videodrome: When he acquires a different kind of programming for his station, a sleazy cable-TV programmer begins to see his life and the future of media spin out of control in a terrifying new reality. Director: David Cronenberg - Stars: James Woods, Debbie Harry, Sonja Smits, Peter Dvorsky

20. The Right Stuff: The story of the original Mercury 7 astronauts and their macho, seat-of-the-pants approach to the space program. Director: Philip Kaufman - Stars: Sam Shepard, Scott Glenn, Ed Harris, Dennis Quaid. Gross: $21.50M

21. Krull: A prince and a fellowship of companions set out to rescue his bride from a fortress of alien invaders who have arrived on their home planet. Director: Peter Yates - Stars: Ken Marshall, Lysette Anthony, Freddie Jones, Francesca Annis

22. The Big Chill: A group of seven former college friends gather for a weekend reunion at a South Carolina winter house after the funeral of one of their friends. Director: Lawrence Kasdan - Stars: Tom Berenger, Glenn Close, Jeff Goldblum, William Hurt. Gross: $56.40M

23. Class: A young man in private school spends one crazy night out, but soon realizes the woman he hooked up with is not who he expected. Director: Lewis John Carlino - Stars: Jacqueline Bisset, Rob Lowe, Andrew McCarthy, Cliff Robertson

24. Sleepaway Camp: Angela Baker, a traumatized and very shy young girl, is sent to summer camp with her cousin. Shortly after her arrival, anyone with sinister or less than honorable intentions gets their comeuppance. Director: Robert Hiltzik - Stars: Felissa Rose, Jonathan Tiersten, Karen Fields, Christopher Collet

25. Valley Girl: Julie, a girl from the valley, meets Randy, a punk from the city. They are from different worlds and find love. Somehow they need to stay together in spite of her trendy, shallow friends. Director: Martha Coolidge - Stars: Nicolas Cage, Deborah Foreman, Elizabeth Daily, Michael Bowen.

In Conclusion:

Thank you for reading my book. I hope you enjoyed it. If this book is successful (it is the first of this style I have published) then I will put out other books spotlighting major years in pro wrestling history. I have compiled a very substantial timeline of pro wrestling history at When It Was Cool under the section: *The Ultimate History of Pro Wrestling Timeline*.

I also hope you will consider subscribing to our various podcasts on the When It Was Cool Podcasting Network including: When It Was Cool Wrestling (where I talk in detail about the history of professional wrestling), When It Was Cool Retro (which reviews movies, TV, comics, music, toys, and other retro pop culture properties), When It Was Cool Dark (where we examine mysteries and dark events in pop culture, and the Wrestling With the Dawg Podcast by Eric Darsie which is also a history-centric pro wrestling podcast.

You can best support us by becoming a Patreon supporter at WhenItWasCool.com. Just click any of the Patreon buttons and sign up and, starting at $1 per month, you can get instant access to over 2000 podcasts about pro wrestling history and retro pop culture. That is our primary way we keep our website, podcast network, and now our publishing division active. Without it, we could not be here. I think you'll find it a fun and informative place and a very positive community.